Mometrix
TEST PREPARATION

I0880289

CPA

Auditing & Attestation Exam Secrets Study Guide

Dear Future Exam Success Story

First of all, **THANK YOU** for purchasing Mometrix study materials!

Second, congratulations! You are one of the few determined test-takers who are committed to doing whatever it takes to excel on your exam. **You have come to the right place.** We developed these study materials with one goal in mind: to deliver you the information you need in a format that's concise and easy to use.

In addition to optimizing your guide for the content of the test, we've outlined our recommended steps for breaking down the preparation process into small, attainable goals so you can make sure you stay on track.

We've also analyzed the entire test-taking process, identifying the most common pitfalls and showing how you can overcome them and be ready for any curveball the test throws you.

Standardized testing is one of the biggest obstacles on your road to success, which only increases the importance of doing well in the high-pressure, high-stakes environment of test day. Your results on this test could have a significant impact on your future, and this guide provides the information and practical advice to help you achieve your full potential on test day.

Your success is our success

We would love to hear from you! If you would like to share the story of your exam success or if you have any questions or comments in regard to our products, please contact us at **800-673-8175** or **support@mometrix.com**.

Thanks again for your business and we wish you continued success!

Sincerely,
The Mometrix Test Preparation Team

Need more help? Check out our flashcards at:
http://MometrixFlashcards.com/CPA

Written and edited by the Mometrix Exam Secrets Test Prep Team
Printed in the United States of America

Table of Contents

Introduction

Thank you for purchasing this resource! You have made the choice to prepare yourself for a test that could have a huge impact on your future, and this guide is designed to help you be fully ready for test day. Obviously, it's important to have a solid understanding of the test material, but you also need to be prepared for the unique environment and stressors of the test, so that you can perform to the best of your abilities.

For this purpose, the first section that appears in this guide is the **Secret Keys**. We've devoted countless hours to meticulously researching what works and what doesn't, and we've boiled down our findings to the five most impactful steps you can take to improve your performance on the test. We start at the beginning with study planning and move through the preparation process, all the way to the testing strategies that will help you get the most out of what you know when you're finally sitting in front of the test.

We recommend that you start preparing for your test as far in advance as possible. However, if you've bought this guide as a last-minute study resource and only have a few days before your test, we recommend that you skip over the first two Secret Keys since they address a long-term study plan.

If you struggle with **test anxiety**, we strongly encourage you to check out our recommendations for how you can overcome it. Test anxiety is a formidable foe, but it can be beaten, and we want to make sure you have the tools you need to defeat it.

Secret Key #1 – Plan Big, Study Small

There's a lot riding on your performance. If you want to ace this test, you're going to need to keep your skills sharp and the material fresh in your mind. You need a plan that lets you review everything you need to know while still fitting in your schedule. We'll break this strategy down into three categories.

Information Organization

Start with the information you already have: the official test outline. From this, you can make a complete list of all the concepts you need to cover before the test. Organize these concepts into groups that can be studied together, and create a list of any related vocabulary you need to learn so you can brush up on any difficult terms. You'll want to keep this vocabulary list handy once you actually start studying since you may need to add to it along the way.

Time Management

Once you have your set of study concepts, decide how to spread them out over the time you have left before the test. Break your study plan into small, clear goals so you have a manageable task for each day and know exactly what you're doing. Then just focus on one small step at a time. When you manage your time this way, you don't need to spend hours at a time studying. Studying a small block of content for a short period each day helps you retain information better and avoid stressing over how much you have left to do. You can relax knowing that you have a plan to cover everything in time. In order for this strategy to be effective though, you have to start studying early and stick to your schedule. Avoid the exhaustion and futility that comes from last-minute cramming!

Study Environment

The environment you study in has a big impact on your learning. Studying in a coffee shop, while probably more enjoyable, is not likely to be as fruitful as studying in a quiet room. It's important to keep distractions to a minimum. You're only planning to study for a short block of time, so make the most of it. Don't pause to check your phone or get up to find a snack. It's also important to **avoid multitasking**. Research has consistently shown that multitasking will make your studying dramatically less effective. Your study area should also be comfortable and well-lit so you don't have the distraction of straining your eyes or sitting on an uncomfortable chair.

The time of day you study is also important. You want to be rested and alert. Don't wait until just before bedtime. Study when you'll be most likely to comprehend and remember. Even better, if you know what time of day your test will be, set that time aside for study. That way your brain will be used to working on that subject at that specific time and you'll have a better chance of recalling information.

Finally, it can be helpful to team up with others who are studying for the same test. Your actual studying should be done in as isolated an environment as possible, but the work of organizing the information and setting up the study plan can be divided up. In between study sessions, you can discuss with your teammates the concepts that you're all studying and quiz each other on the details. Just be sure that your teammates are as serious about the test as you are. If you find that your study time is being replaced with social time, you might need to find a new team.

Secret Key #2 – Make Your Studying Count

You're devoting a lot of time and effort to preparing for this test, so you want to be absolutely certain it will pay off. This means doing more than just reading the content and hoping you can remember it on test day. It's important to make every minute of study count. There are two main areas you can focus on to make your studying count.

Retention

It doesn't matter how much time you study if you can't remember the material. You need to make sure you are retaining the concepts. To check your retention of the information you're learning, try recalling it at later times with minimal prompting. Try carrying around flashcards and glance at one or two from time to time or ask a friend who's also studying for the test to quiz you.

To enhance your retention, look for ways to put the information into practice so that you can apply it rather than simply recalling it. If you're using the information in practical ways, it will be much easier to remember. Similarly, it helps to solidify a concept in your mind if you're not only reading it to yourself but also explaining it to someone else. Ask a friend to let you teach them about a concept you're a little shaky on (or speak aloud to an imaginary audience if necessary). As you try to summarize, define, give examples, and answer your friend's questions, you'll understand the concepts better and they will stay with you longer. Finally, step back for a big picture view and ask yourself how each piece of information fits with the whole subject. When you link the different concepts together and see them working together as a whole, it's easier to remember the individual components.

Finally, practice showing your work on any multi-step problems, even if you're just studying. Writing out each step you take to solve a problem will help solidify the process in your mind, and you'll be more likely to remember it during the test.

Modality

Modality simply refers to the means or method by which you study. Choosing a study modality that fits your own individual learning style is crucial. No two people learn best in exactly the same way, so it's important to know your strengths and use them to your advantage.

For example, if you learn best by visualization, focus on visualizing a concept in your mind and draw an image or a diagram. Try color-coding your notes, illustrating them, or creating symbols that will trigger your mind to recall a learned concept. If you learn best by hearing or discussing information, find a study partner who learns the same way or read aloud to yourself. Think about how to put the information in your own words. Imagine that you are giving a lecture on the topic and record yourself so you can listen to it later.

For any learning style, flashcards can be helpful. Organize the information so you can take advantage of spare moments to review. Underline key words or phrases. Use different colors for different categories. Mnemonic devices (such as creating a short list in which every item starts with the same letter) can also help with retention. Find what works best for you and use it to store the information in your mind most effectively and easily.

Secret Key #3 – Practice the Right Way

Your success on test day depends not only on how many hours you put into preparing, but also on whether you prepared the right way. It's good to check along the way to see if your studying is paying off. One of the most effective ways to do this is by taking practice tests to evaluate your progress. Practice tests are useful because they show exactly where you need to improve. Every time you take a practice test, pay special attention to these three groups of questions:

- The questions you got wrong
- The questions you had to guess on, even if you guessed right
- The questions you found difficult or slow to work through

This will show you exactly what your weak areas are, and where you need to devote more study time. Ask yourself why each of these questions gave you trouble. Was it because you didn't understand the material? Was it because you didn't remember the vocabulary? Do you need more repetitions on this type of question to build speed and confidence? Dig into those questions and figure out how you can strengthen your weak areas as you go back to review the material.

Additionally, many practice tests have a section explaining the answer choices. It can be tempting to read the explanation and think that you now have a good understanding of the concept. However, an explanation likely only covers part of the question's broader context. Even if the explanation makes perfect sense, **go back and investigate** every concept related to the question until you're positive you have a thorough understanding.

As you go along, keep in mind that the practice test is just that: practice. Memorizing these questions and answers will not be very helpful on the actual test because it is unlikely to have any of the same exact questions. If you only know the right answers to the sample questions, you won't be prepared for the real thing. **Study the concepts** until you understand them fully, and then you'll be able to answer any question that shows up on the test.

It's important to wait on the practice tests until you're ready. If you take a test on your first day of study, you may be overwhelmed by the amount of material covered and how much you need to learn. Work up to it gradually.

On test day, you'll need to be prepared for answering questions, managing your time, and using the test-taking strategies you've learned. It's a lot to balance, like a mental marathon that will have a big impact on your future. Like training for a marathon, you'll need to start slowly and work your way up. When test day arrives, you'll be ready.

Start with the strategies you've read in the first two Secret Keys—plan your course and study in the way that works best for you. If you have time, consider using multiple study resources to get different approaches to the same concepts. It can be helpful to see difficult concepts from more than one angle. Then find a good source for practice tests. Many times, the test website will suggest potential study resources or provide sample tests.

Practice Test Strategy

If you're able to find at least three practice tests, we recommend this strategy:

Untimed and Open-Book Practice

Take the first test with no time constraints and with your notes and study guide handy. Take your time and focus on applying the strategies you've learned.

Timed and Open-Book Practice

Take the second practice test open-book as well, but set a timer and practice pacing yourself to finish in time.

Timed and Closed-Book Practice

Take any other practice tests as if it were test day. Set a timer and put away your study materials. Sit at a table or desk in a quiet room, imagine yourself at the testing center, and answer questions as quickly and accurately as possible.

Keep repeating timed and closed-book tests on a regular basis until you run out of practice tests or it's time for the actual test. Your mind will be ready for the schedule and stress of test day, and you'll be able to focus on recalling the material you've learned.

Secret Key #4 – Pace Yourself

Once you're fully prepared for the material on the test, your biggest challenge on test day will be managing your time. Just knowing that the clock is ticking can make you panic even if you have plenty of time left. Work on pacing yourself so you can build confidence against the time constraints of the exam. Pacing is a difficult skill to master, especially in a high-pressure environment, so **practice is vital**.

Set time expectations for your pace based on how much time is available. For example, if a section has 60 questions and the time limit is 30 minutes, you know you have to average 30 seconds or less per question in order to answer them all. Although 30 seconds is the hard limit, set 25 seconds per question as your goal, so you reserve extra time to spend on harder questions. When you budget extra time for the harder questions, you no longer have any reason to stress when those questions take longer to answer.

Don't let this time expectation distract you from working through the test at a calm, steady pace, but keep it in mind so you don't spend too much time on any one question. Recognize that taking extra time on one question you don't understand may keep you from answering two that you do understand later in the test. If your time limit for a question is up and you're still not sure of the answer, mark it and move on, and come back to it later if the time and the test format allow. If the testing format doesn't allow you to return to earlier questions, just make an educated guess; then put it out of your mind and move on.

On the easier questions, be careful not to rush. It may seem wise to hurry through them so you have more time for the challenging ones, but it's not worth missing one if you know the concept and just didn't take the time to read the question fully. Work efficiently but make sure you understand the question and have looked at all of the answer choices, since more than one may seem right at first.

Even if you're paying attention to the time, you may find yourself a little behind at some point. You should speed up to get back on track, but do so wisely. Don't panic; just take a few seconds less on each question until you're caught up. Don't guess without thinking, but do look through the answer choices and eliminate any you know are wrong. If you can get down to two choices, it is often worthwhile to guess from those. Once you've chosen an answer, move on and don't dwell on any that you skipped or had to hurry through. If a question was taking too long, chances are it was one of the harder ones, so you weren't as likely to get it right anyway.

On the other hand, if you find yourself getting ahead of schedule, it may be beneficial to slow down a little. The more quickly you work, the more likely you are to make a careless mistake that will affect your score. You've budgeted time for each question, so don't be afraid to spend that time. Practice an efficient but careful pace to get the most out of the time you have.

Secret Key #5 – Have a Plan for Guessing

When you're taking the test, you may find yourself stuck on a question. Some of the answer choices seem better than others, but you don't see the one answer choice that is obviously correct. What do you do?

The scenario described above is very common, yet most test takers have not effectively prepared for it. Developing and practicing a plan for guessing may be one of the single most effective uses of your time as you get ready for the exam.

In developing your plan for guessing, there are three questions to address:

- When should you start the guessing process?
- How should you narrow down the choices?
- Which answer should you choose?

When to Start the Guessing Process

Unless your plan for guessing is to select C every time (which, despite its merits, is not what we recommend), you need to leave yourself enough time to apply your answer elimination strategies. Since you have a limited amount of time for each question, that means that if you're going to give yourself the best shot at guessing correctly, you have to decide quickly whether or not you will guess.

Of course, the best-case scenario is that you don't have to guess at all, so first, see if you can answer the question based on your knowledge of the subject and basic reasoning skills. Focus on the key words in the question and try to jog your memory of related topics. Give yourself a chance to bring the knowledge to mind, but once you realize that you don't have (or you can't access) the knowledge you need to answer the question, it's time to start the guessing process.

It's almost always better to start the guessing process too early than too late. It only takes a few seconds to remember something and answer the question from knowledge. Carefully eliminating wrong answer choices takes longer. Plus, going through the process of eliminating answer choices can actually help jog your memory.

Summary: Start the guessing process as soon as you decide that you can't answer the question based on your knowledge.

How to Narrow Down the Choices

The next chapter in this book (**Test-Taking Strategies**) includes a wide range of strategies for how to approach questions and how to look for answer choices to eliminate. You will definitely want to read those carefully, practice them, and figure out which ones work best for you. Here though, we're going to address a mindset rather than a particular strategy.

Your odds of guessing an answer correctly depend on how many options you are choosing from.

Number of options left	5	4	3	2	1
Odds of guessing correctly	20%	25%	33%	50%	100%

You can see from this chart just how valuable it is to be able to eliminate incorrect answers and make an educated guess, but there are two things that many test takers do that cause them to miss out on the benefits of guessing:

- Accidentally eliminating the correct answer
- Selecting an answer based on an impression

We'll look at the first one here, and the second one in the next section.

To avoid accidentally eliminating the correct answer, we recommend a thought exercise called **the $5 challenge**. In this challenge, you only eliminate an answer choice from contention if you are willing to bet $5 on it being wrong. Why $5? Five dollars is a small but not insignificant amount of money. It's an amount you could afford to lose but wouldn't want to throw away. And while losing $5 once might not hurt too much, doing it twenty times will set you back $100. In the same way, each small decision you make—eliminating a choice here, guessing on a question there—won't by itself impact your score very much, but when you put them all together, they can make a big difference. By holding each answer choice elimination decision to a higher standard, you can reduce the risk of accidentally eliminating the correct answer.

The $5 challenge can also be applied in a positive sense: If you are willing to bet $5 that an answer choice *is* correct, go ahead and mark it as correct.

Summary: Only eliminate an answer choice if you are willing to bet $5 that it is wrong.

Which Answer to Choose

You're taking the test. You've run into a hard question and decided you'll have to guess. You've eliminated all the answer choices you're willing to bet $5 on. Now you have to pick an answer. Why do we even need to talk about this? Why can't you just pick whichever one you feel like when the time comes?

The answer to these questions is that if you don't come into the test with a plan, you'll rely on your impression to select an answer choice, and if you do that, you risk falling into a trap. The test writers know that everyone who takes their test will be guessing on some of the questions, so they intentionally write wrong answer choices to seem plausible. You still have to pick an answer though, and if the wrong answer choices are designed to look right, how can you ever be sure that you're not falling for their trap? The best solution we've found to this dilemma is to take the decision out of your hands entirely. Here is the process we recommend:

Once you've eliminated any choices that you are confident (willing to bet $5) are wrong, select the first remaining choice as your answer.

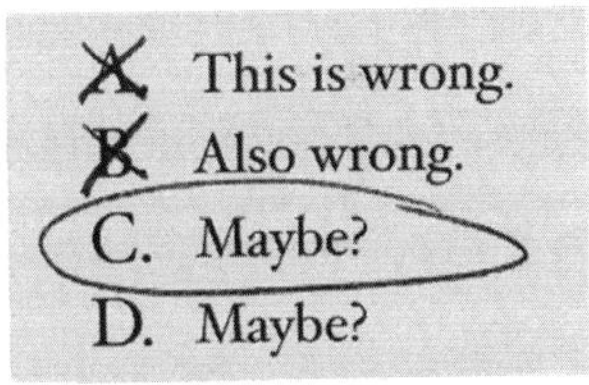

Whether you choose to select the first remaining choice, the second, or the last, the important thing is that you use some preselected standard. Using this approach guarantees that you will not be enticed into selecting an answer choice that looks right, because you are not basing your decision on how the answer choices look.

This is not meant to make you question your knowledge. Instead, it is to help you recognize the difference between your knowledge and your impressions. There's a huge difference between thinking an answer is right because of what you know, and thinking an answer is right because it looks or sounds like it should be right.

Summary: To ensure that your selection is appropriately random, make a predetermined selection from among all answer choices you have not eliminated.

Test-Taking Strategies

This section contains a list of test-taking strategies that you may find helpful as you work through the test. By taking what you know and applying logical thought, you can maximize your chances of answering any question correctly!

It is very important to realize that every question is different and every person is different: no single strategy will work on every question, and no single strategy will work for every person. That's why we've included all of them here, so you can try them out and determine which ones work best for different types of questions and which ones work best for you.

Question Strategies

☑ Read Carefully

Read the question and the answer choices carefully. Don't miss the question because you misread the terms. You have plenty of time to read each question thoroughly and make sure you understand what is being asked. Yet a happy medium must be attained, so don't waste too much time. You must read carefully and efficiently.

☑ Contextual Clues

Look for contextual clues. If the question includes a word you are not familiar with, look at the immediate context for some indication of what the word might mean. Contextual clues can often give you all the information you need to decipher the meaning of an unfamiliar word. Even if you can't determine the meaning, you may be able to narrow down the possibilities enough to make a solid guess at the answer to the question.

☑ Prefixes

If you're having trouble with a word in the question or answer choices, try dissecting it. Take advantage of every clue that the word might include. Prefixes can be a huge help. Usually, they allow you to determine a basic meaning. *Pre-* means before, *post-* means after, *pro-* is positive, *de-* is negative. From prefixes, you can get an idea of the general meaning of the word and try to put it into context.

☑ Hedge Words

Watch out for critical hedge words, such as *likely, may, can, often, almost, mostly, usually, generally, rarely*, and *sometimes*. Question writers insert these hedge phrases to cover every possibility. Often an answer choice will be wrong simply because it leaves no room for exception. Be on guard for answer choices that have definitive words such as *exactly* and *always*.

☑ Switchback Words

Stay alert for *switchbacks*. These are the words and phrases frequently used to alert you to shifts in thought. The most common switchback words are *but, although*, and *however*. Others include *nevertheless, on the other hand, even though, while, in spite of, despite*, and *regardless of*. Switchback words are important to catch because they can change the direction of the question or an answer choice.

☑ FACE VALUE

When in doubt, use common sense. Accept the situation in the problem at face value. Don't read too much into it. These problems will not require you to make wild assumptions. If you have to go beyond creativity and warp time or space in order to have an answer choice fit the question, then you should move on and consider the other answer choices. These are normal problems rooted in reality. The applicable relationship or explanation may not be readily apparent, but it is there for you to figure out. Use your common sense to interpret anything that isn't clear.

Answer Choice Strategies

☑ ANSWER SELECTION

The most thorough way to pick an answer choice is to identify and eliminate wrong answers until only one is left, then confirm it is the correct answer. Sometimes an answer choice may immediately seem right, but be careful. The test writers will usually put more than one reasonable answer choice on each question, so take a second to read all of them and make sure that the other choices are not equally obvious. As long as you have time left, it is better to read every answer choice than to pick the first one that looks right without checking the others.

☑ ANSWER CHOICE FAMILIES

An answer choice family consists of two (in rare cases, three) answer choices that are very similar in construction and cannot all be true at the same time. If you see two answer choices that are direct opposites or parallels, one of them is usually the correct answer. For instance, if one answer choice says that quantity *x* increases and another either says that quantity *x* decreases (opposite) or says that quantity *y* increases (parallel), then those answer choices would fall into the same family. An answer choice that doesn't match the construction of the answer choice family is more likely to be incorrect. Most questions will not have answer choice families, but when they do appear, you should be prepared to recognize them.

☑ ELIMINATE ANSWERS

Eliminate answer choices as soon as you realize they are wrong, but make sure you consider all possibilities. If you are eliminating answer choices and realize that the last one you are left with is also wrong, don't panic. Start over and consider each choice again. There may be something you missed the first time that you will realize on the second pass.

☑ AVOID FACT TRAPS

Don't be distracted by an answer choice that is factually true but doesn't answer the question. You are looking for the choice that answers the question. Stay focused on what the question is asking for so you don't accidentally pick an answer that is true but incorrect. Always go back to the question and make sure the answer choice you've selected actually answers the question and is not merely a true statement.

☑ EXTREME STATEMENTS

In general, you should avoid answers that put forth extreme actions as standard practice or proclaim controversial ideas as established fact. An answer choice that states the "process should be used in certain situations, if..." is much more likely to be correct than one that states the "process should be discontinued completely." The first is a calm rational statement and doesn't even make a definitive, uncompromising stance, using a hedge word *if* to provide wiggle room, whereas the second choice is far more extreme.

✓ Benchmark

As you read through the answer choices and you come across one that seems to answer the question well, mentally select that answer choice. This is not your final answer, but it's the one that will help you evaluate the other answer choices. The one that you selected is your benchmark or standard for judging each of the other answer choices. Every other answer choice must be compared to your benchmark. That choice is correct until proven otherwise by another answer choice beating it. If you find a better answer, then that one becomes your new benchmark. Once you've decided that no other choice answers the question as well as your benchmark, you have your final answer.

✓ Predict the Answer

Before you even start looking at the answer choices, it is often best to try to predict the answer. When you come up with the answer on your own, it is easier to avoid distractions and traps because you will know exactly what to look for. The right answer choice is unlikely to be word-for-word what you came up with, but it should be a close match. Even if you are confident that you have the right answer, you should still take the time to read each option before moving on.

General Strategies

✓ Tough Questions

If you are stumped on a problem or it appears too hard or too difficult, don't waste time. Move on! Remember though, if you can quickly check for obviously incorrect answer choices, your chances of guessing correctly are greatly improved. Before you completely give up, at least try to knock out a couple of possible answers. Eliminate what you can and then guess at the remaining answer choices before moving on.

✓ Check Your Work

Since you will probably not know every term listed and the answer to every question, it is important that you get credit for the ones that you do know. Don't miss any questions through careless mistakes. If at all possible, try to take a second to look back over your answer selection and make sure you've selected the correct answer choice and haven't made a costly careless mistake (such as marking an answer choice that you didn't mean to mark). This quick double check should more than pay for itself in caught mistakes for the time it costs.

✓ Pace Yourself

It's easy to be overwhelmed when you're looking at a page full of questions; your mind is confused and full of random thoughts, and the clock is ticking down faster than you would like. Calm down and maintain the pace that you have set for yourself. Especially as you get down to the last few minutes of the test, don't let the small numbers on the clock make you panic. As long as you are on track by monitoring your pace, you are guaranteed to have time for each question.

✓ Don't Rush

It is very easy to make errors when you are in a hurry. Maintaining a fast pace in answering questions is pointless if it makes you miss questions that you would have gotten right otherwise. Test writers like to include distracting information and wrong answers that seem right. Taking a little extra time to avoid careless mistakes can make all the difference in your test score. Find a pace that allows you to be confident in the answers that you select.

⊘ KEEP MOVING

Panicking will not help you pass the test, so do your best to stay calm and keep moving. Taking deep breaths and going through the answer elimination steps you practiced can help to break through a stress barrier and keep your pace.

Final Notes

The combination of a solid foundation of content knowledge and the confidence that comes from practicing your plan for applying that knowledge is the key to maximizing your performance on test day. As your foundation of content knowledge is built up and strengthened, you'll find that the strategies included in this chapter become more and more effective in helping you quickly sift through the distractions and traps of the test to isolate the correct answer.

Now that you're preparing to move forward into the test content chapters of this book, be sure to keep your goal in mind. As you read, think about how you will be able to apply this information on the test. If you've already seen sample questions for the test and you have an idea of the question format and style, try to come up with questions of your own that you can answer based on what you're reading. This will give you valuable practice applying your knowledge in the same ways you can expect to on test day.

Good luck and good studying!

Engagement Acceptance

Phases of an Audit

Phases of an Audit:

1. Plan and design the audit approach
    a. Obtain background information
    b. Obtain information about client's obligations
    c. Preliminary analytical procedures
    d. Initial risk assessments
    e. Understand internal control and assess control risk
    f. Develop the audit program (procedures, sample size, items to select, timing)
2. Perform tests of controls and substantive tests of transactions
3. Perform analytical procedures and tests of details of balances
4. Complete the audit and issue an audit report
    a. The **objective of the independent audit** is to provide reasonable assurance that the financial statements are free of material misstatements. The CPA expresses an opinion on the fairness with which the financial statements present cash flows and results of operations. The independent audit is important to financial statement readers because it involves the objective examination of, and reporting on, management-prepared financial statements.

Nature and Scope of an Auditing Engagement

When determining the scope of an auditing engagement, the auditor should seek to understand the basis of reporting, reporting requirements that are specific to the industry, and the place(s) where the organization is located. The auditor should also grasp relations between parents and subsidiaries for the organization, the role of internal auditors, the necessity of specialized knowledge, the role of information technology on audit procedures, and the access he can have to client personnel and data.

- Further, to determine the nature of the engagement, the auditor should seek to learn more preliminary information about the company, such as areas where there is a higher risk of material misstatement, accounts or sections which are more material than others, and substantial developments affected the organization's obligations for financial reporting or other matters.
- In sum, the auditor needs to learn a lot about the company that he is thinking about auditing. In doing so, he can formulate a general plan of how the auditing engagement will look.

Types of Audits

Various Opinions for Audit Reports, Audit Objectives, and Auditing Standards

Financial audits are when an independent certified public accountant examines a client's accounting records to develop an audit opinion. The auditor will review source documents to verify transactions and will also assess internal control.

Internal audits occur when an internal auditor examines company activities to verify that they are in agreement with company policy, regulations, a reporting framework (e.g. GAAP), or other relevant standards.

Management audits are assessments of the efficiency of management.

Compliance audits provide verification that the firm is in compliance with designated guidelines.

Types of audit opinions:

1. Unqualified/unmodified opinion
2. Qualified/modified opinion
3. Adverse opinion
4. Disclaimer

Audit objectives are broad statements developed by internal auditors which define intended audit accomplishments. Audit objectives can be transaction-related (general and specific) or balance-related (general and specific).

Auditing standards measure audit performance quality.

PURPOSE OF AUDIT PLANNING AND ELEMENTS OF PREPLANNING

The purpose of audit planning is to enhance audit efficiency and effectiveness.

Preplanning directions to the auditor:

- Determine new client acceptance and continuance. Identify client's reasons for audit. Determine audit staffing. Determine agreement with client by use of an engagement letter, which should contain the engagement goals, responsibilities of management, responsibilities of the auditor, and any audit limitations.
- Obtain knowledge of client's industry and business.
- Understand the client's business. The auditor should understand the impact of general economic factors on the client's industry, such as inflation, consumer demands, and environmental issues.
- Consider the use of specialists, who are persons skilled in fields other than accounting and auditing. Auditors must know about the professional qualifications and reputation, specialists should be unrelated to company under audit, and the auditor must obtain an understanding of specialist's methods and assumptions. Provided some additional auditing work is done on the accounting information used by the specialists, the auditor may rely on their work in connection with his audit decisions.

TYPES OF CPA ATTESTATION ENGAGEMENTS

In **examinations**, supporting documentation, procedures, and employees are examined to assure the accuracy of a company's financial records for an audit. These will typically conclude with a positive opinion. An **audit** is a type of examination.

In a **review** for a nonpublic company, auditors will use inquiry and analytical procedures to provide negative (or limited) assurance that the auditor has no knowledge of the financial statements not being materially in agreement with the applicable reporting framework. In reviews, audit evidence and internal control are not examined. A review is less comprehensive in scope than an audit. Independence is required for a review.

Agreed-upon procedures are performed and completed in accordance with attestation standards, and the findings are reported.

A **compilation** is conducted for a nonpublic company. The accountant does not express any assurance or opinion on the financial statements.

For **unaudited financial statements**, an accountant prepares the financial statements but does not examine them in accordance with generally accepted auditing standards (GAAS). Audit procedures are not performed to provide an opinion. The accountant must provide a disclaimer that no opinion is given.

Note: If a CPA is engaged to conduct more than one service, the only report issued is the one for the highest level of service.

GOVERNMENTAL AUDITING

Audits are categorized into two groups by GAS: **performance** and **financial**. The auditor should report illegal acts discovered during the audit to the Federal Inspector General if management does not report illegal acts to the grantor or take corrective action.

1. For **GAAS audits**, GAS and Single Audit laws do not apply to the entity. The audit procedures must follow GAAS guidelines, and an opinion must be issued on the financial statements.
2. For **GAS (Governmental Auditing Standards or "yellow book") audits**, the auditor must report on the financial statements, internal control, and compliance with laws and regulations. The audit procedures parallel with GAAS audits.
   a. In cases of **noncompliance** (cases in which laws and regulations are not followed that could possibly result in a material misstatement of the financial statements), internal control must be written and must include information about the auditor's test work, any internal control deficiencies, and material reportable conditions that may exist.
3. The **Single Audit Act of 1984** requires audits of entities that expend $500,000 or more of federal assistance received for operations. The audit is conducted in accordance with Generally Accepted Government Auditing Standards (GAGAS), using the guidance provided by OMB Circular A-133 and its Compliance Supplement.

OPINION TYPES FOR DEPARTURES FROM GAAP

Departures from GAAP (or whatever the applicable reporting framework is) can lead to a **modified opinion** or an **adverse opinion**, depending on the materiality. A less material departure would cause a modified/qualified opinion; a more material departure would cause an adverse opinion. Either of these opinions requires an additional paragraph before the opinion paragraph.

An example of a departure from GAAP would be the client's treating a capital lease as an operating lease. An omission of the statement of cash flows is a departure from GAAP resulting in a modified opinion due to inadequate disclosure; the audit report would include a paragraph explaining that the company declined to present the required statement. Should a client be required to disclose segment disclosures and either omit or disclose incorrect segment disclosures, a modified or adverse opinion would be given. When auditing a public entity's financial statements that include segment information, the auditor should audit the segment information and, if the information is adequate and in conformity with GAAP, not make reference to the segment information in the auditor's report.

UNMODIFIED OPINION

There are cases in which an auditor will issue a standard unmodified report with an additional paragraph (either an emphasis-of-matter or other-matter paragraph) due to a departure from

GAAP in the financial statements. If the client can justify the departure from GAAP, then it is acceptable, and if the financial statements would be misleading should the client follow GAAP, then it would be justifiable to depart from GAAP.

The lack of consistency in GAAP application between accounting periods can lead to the auditor issuing an unmodified opinion with an additional paragraph. For example, an accounting principle change will affect the comparability of financial statements; if there is a material difference, the auditor will disclose the information in an emphasis-of-matter paragraph. Additionally, changes in business entities and changes in continuing subsidiaries carrying bases, for equity, cost, or consolidated methods, will cause an unmodified opinion with an additional paragraph.

Subsidiary purchases and dispositions do not need to be disclosed in an additional paragraph. Similarly, changes in accounting estimates, corrections of accounting principle errors, and insignificant reclassifications of accounts between years do not require such a paragraph.

Adverse Opinion or Disclaimer of Opinion

A lack of independence can result in a one-paragraph disclaimer being issued.

- A significant going concern can result in a disclaimer with an altered introductory paragraph, altered scope paragraph, altered opinion paragraph, and additional paragraph being added.
- A disclaimer of opinion with an altered introductory paragraph, altered opinion paragraph, and additional paragraph is issued for a significant scope limitation. The scope paragraph is omitted.
- The use of a disclaimer of opinion might indicate that the auditor is so uncertain with respect to an item that the auditor cannot form an opinion on the fairness of presentation of the financial statements as a whole.
- The use of an adverse opinion generally indicates a violation of the framework so material that a modified opinion is not justified, much less an unmodified opinion. The opinion paragraph is altered and a paragraph is added for explanation.

Misleading Financial Statements

The standard US unmodified audit report states that the audited financial statements present fairly, in all material respects, an entity's financial position, results of operations, and cash flows, in conformity with the applicable reporting framework (e.g. GAAP). An auditor should not express an unmodified audit opinion if the financial statements contain a material departure from the framework unless, due to unusual circumstances, adherence to the framework would make them misleading.

The CPA's reporting responsibilities are not met by attaching an explanation of the circumstances and a disclaimer of opinion to financial statements if the CPA believes that the financial statements are false or misleading.

Client-Imposed Scope Limitations

If the **scope limitation** is caused by the client and the limitation is significant in the scope of the audit, the auditor will need to generally disclaim. If the client-imposed limitation is not significant and the auditor cannot find alternative methods of testing, the auditor will issue a modified opinion or disclaimer.

For example, restrictions imposed by a client prohibit the confirmation of accounts receivable by direct communication with debtors. These receivables account for 30% of all assets and alternate audit procedures can not be applied, although the independent auditor was able to examine satisfactory evidence for all other items in the financial statements. The independent auditor should issue a disclaimer of opinion.

An independent auditor is engaged to audit the financial statements of a company one month after its fiscal year had ended. Although the inventory count was not observed by the auditor, and accounts receivable were not confirmed by direct communication with debtors, the auditor was able to gain satisfaction by applying alternate auditing procedures. The audit report will probably contain a standard unmodified opinion.

Preliminary Engagement Activities

Preliminary engagement activities are procedures which the auditor ought to perform at the beginning of his audit engagement, and they should be included in a CPA firm's quality control system. These procedures include an assessment of the client relationship as it is and as it will continue for the specific audit engagement and an inquiry concerning the auditor's conformity with ethical standards, such as independence. The purpose of performing these procedures is to ensure the integrity of both the auditor and management and to clear up any misunderstandings which might exist within the client relationship.

Acceptance and Continuance of Auditing Clients

CPA firms should have a system of quality control in place for the acceptance and continuance of auditing clients, with a number of distinct criteria to apply to decisions of beginning or continuing client relationships and of performing specific engagements for one's clients. The goals of these quality control criteria is to give the firm reasonable assurance that client management has ethical and business integrity, that engagements can be accomplished effectively and with professional expertise, that risks pertinent to a client or engagement are clarified and considered, and that there is mutual understanding between the firm and the client over the auditing services to be performed.

Acquiring a New Client

CPA firms should establish a policy for determining whether or not to accept a new client to prevent becoming associated with a company that lacks integrity in business dealings. Before accepting a new client, a CPA firm should communicate with the predecessor auditor. The firm should acquire as much information as possible about the potential new client before developing an agreement with the new client. Regarding communications with the predecessor auditor, it is the responsibility of the successor auditor to get permission from the client and initiate contact with the predecessor auditor. If the potential new client is reluctant to grant permission to the successor auditor to contact the predecessor auditor, the successor should make all attempts to find out the cause; in this situation, the successor auditor should consider the situation carefully before accepting the new client.

Communications with the predecessor auditor should cover the predecessor's knowledge of the reasons for the auditor change, the management's honesty, any significant disputes between the predecessor and management, especially concerning accounting or auditing, and any communications with the audit committee for fraud, internal control issues, or illegal acts.

Engagement Letter

An **engagement letter** is a letter written by the auditor to the client citing the accounting functions to be performed, responsibilities assumed, the basis for billing, expense reimbursement, and other things. The auditor will usually request that the client sign the engagement letter showing agreement with the terms. The objective of the engagement letter is to obtain a clear agreement between the parties regarding the accounting work to be done and related particulars.

Materiality

Materiality is the magnitude of an omission or misstatement of accounting information that makes it probable that the judgment of a reasonable person relying on the information would have been changed or influenced. Materiality is determined by the type of the item and relative amount. For instance, a small theft by a company's CEO would be material. Accountants and auditors want to maintain that financial reports do not contain material misstatements. When planning an audit, materiality is considered to be the largest amount of uncorrected misstatement that could exist in published financial statements, yet be in conformity with GAAP (i.e., not misleading). Auditors make a judgment about materiality (a dollar amount they are willing to live with) and then allocate the amount to the accounts in the financial statements. A rule of thumb is that anything less than 5% is probably not material, and anything greater than 10% is material. Between 5-10% requires judgment. In the audit planning phase, auditors need to decide how much evidence to accumulate for each account in order to be able to state that the audit was planned and performed to obtain "reasonable assurance" about whether the financial statements are "free of material misstatement." The decisions regarding evidence are based on assessments of the different types of risk and quantification of what is considered "material."

Materiality and Risk

Risk is a measure of uncertainty (captured in the audit risk model), the opposite of assurance, whereas **materiality** is a measure of magnitude or size

The purpose in assessing both materiality and risk is to allocate audit effort to the accounts (transactions) that are most likely to contain material misstatements.

Auditors assign a part of the overall planning materiality to each account. The amount assigned is the **tolerable misstatement**, the amount by which an account may be misstated and yet still not cause the financial statements taken as a whole to be materially misleading. A major determining factor of materiality to consider is who will be using the financial statements.

Audit Risk

Audit risk is the risk that an auditor will give an inappropriate opinion on financial statements. The auditing profession has no official standard for an acceptable level of overall audit risk, except that it should be "acceptably low." To obtain "lower" audit risk (i.e. a lower risk of failure), the auditor needs more substantive evidence (indirect relationship), more experienced personnel, and more review of workpapers. Audit risk has a direct relationship with detection risk, as expressed in the formula:

Audit Risk =Inherent Risk * Control Risk * Detection Risk

Inherent risk is the risk that material misstatements have occurred in transactions entering the accounting system assuming no internal controls. "Relative risk" refers to conditions of more or less inherent risk. Audit care and attention should be greater where relative and inherent risks are judged to be higher. Inherent risk has a direct relationship with substantive evidence. A high inherent risk signifies that there is more substantive evidence to accumulate.

Detection risk is the risk that audit procedures (audit evidence) for a segment will fail to detect existing material misstatements. If there is low detection risk, the audit can be planned with high substantive evidence.

Standards of Reporting in Generally Accepted Auditing Standards (GAAS)

GAAP: According to GAAS, the report shall state whether the financial statements are presented in accordance with the applicable reporting framework (e.g. GAAP or IFRS).

Consistency: The report shall identify those circumstances in which such principles have not been consistently observed in the current period in relation to the preceding period.

Disclosure: Informative disclosures in the financial statements are to be regarded as reasonably adequate unless otherwise stated in the report. The primary responsibility for the adequacy of disclosure in the financial statements of a publicly held company rests with the management of the company.

Opinion: The report shall either contain an expression of opinion regarding the financial statements, taken as a whole, or an assertion to the effect that an opinion cannot be expressed. When an overall opinion cannot be expressed, the reasons should be stated. In all cases where an auditor's name is associated with financial statements, the report should contain a clear-cut indication of the character of the auditor's work, if any, and the degree of responsibility the auditor is taking.

General Standards and Standards of Fieldwork of Generally Accepted Auditing Standards (GAAS)

GAAS consists of General Standards, Standards of Fieldwork, and Standards of Reporting.

General Standards:

1. **Training**: The audit is to be performed by a person or persons having adequate technical training and proficiency as an auditor.
2. **Independence**: In all matters relating to the assignment, the auditor or auditors should maintain independence in fact and appearance. The auditors are to be without bias with respect to the client under audit.
3. **Professional Care**: Due professional care is to be exercised in the planning and performance of the audit and the preparation of the report.

Standards of Fieldwork:

1. **Planning**: The work is to be adequately planned and assistants, if any, are to be properly supervised. Assistants' work should be reviewed to ensure accuracy in both the test work and support of the conclusion. This standard acknowledges that early appointment of the auditor is advantageous to the client and the auditor.
2. **Independence**: A sufficient understanding of internal control is to be obtained to plan the audit and to determine the nature, timing, and extent of tests to be performed.
3. **Evidence**: Sufficient competent evidential matter is to be obtained through inspection, observation, inquiries, and confirmations to afford a reasonable basis for an opinion regarding the financial statements.

Hierarchy of Generally Accepted Auditing Standards (GAAS)

The levels of Generally Accepted Auditing Standards (GAAS) are:

1. **Statements on Auditing Standards** (SASs), which are published by the AICPA Auditing Standards Board.
2. **Interpretive publications**, which denote the method in which SASs are to be used. These include AICPA Statements of Position, AICPA Audit and Accounting Guides, SAS appendixes, and Interpretations of SASs.
3. **Miscellaneous publications**, which include Journal of Accountancy auditing articles, AICPA letter auditing articles, textbooks, CPE materials, and other professional journal auditing articles.
    a. Professional judgment should be utilized when applying GAAS. If a CPA departs from SASs or interpretive publications, the CPA should be capable of justifying any departures. Other auditing publications are not considered to have authoritative status.
    b. The Auditing Standards Board of the AICPA has circulated ten Generally Accepted Auditing Standards (GAAS), which must be used by all CPAs to conduct audits. GAAS measures the quality of the auditor's performance.
    c. In June 2008, the Auditing Standards Board eliminated its standard on the hierarchy of generally accepted auditing standards and the Financial Accounting Standards Board issued a new standard establishing the same hierarchy.

Supervision of Auditors' Assistants

It is imperative that an auditor appropriately supervise his auditing assistants. This should include directing the assistants to help them accomplish their tasks and objectives and assessing their work to discern whether they successfully performed their work. The auditor should communicate the assistant's responsibilities and the objectives for the various audit procedures, including the fact that assistants should report to the auditor with any questions, difficulties, or peculiar findings.

Using the Work of Other Independent Auditors

Due to the inefficiency of repeatedly testing the same controls or procedures unnecessarily, it can be proper for auditors to depend upon the work of internal auditors or other external auditors. To determine whether the utilization of others' work would be appropriate, the auditor ought to determine whether his participation is sufficient to qualify himself as the principal auditor. He also ought to determine whether the other auditor is sufficiently competent and independent, whether the work performed by the other auditor is adequate for the principal auditor's use, and what substantial findings the other auditor had, including those findings' effect on the principal auditor's audit opinion.

These conditions are further explained in Internal Standard on Auditing (ISA) 5, "Using the Work of Another Auditor."

Specialists Involved in an Audit

If an auditor selects specialists to aid in an audit engagement, then he should discern whether the specialist will participate as a member of the audit team (e.g. a tax professional could aid with audit procedures), and if so, the auditor should seek to supervise the specialist as an assistant.

Specialists sometimes needed for audit engagements will specialize in information technology. When determining the necessity of an IT specialist, the auditor should duly consider the complexity of the organization's processes, the degree to which data is shared among information systems, the organization's use of recent technologies, the availability of audit evidence in electronic and non-electronic form, and other similar considerations.

Functions of Internal Auditing and the Internal Auditor

Internal auditing is an objective assurance and consulting activity designed to add value and improve an organization's operations. It helps an organization accomplish its objectives by bringing a systematic, disciplined approach to evaluate and improve the effectiveness of risk management, control, and governance processes.

Internal auditors are individuals within an organization's internal auditing department who are assigned the responsibility of performing internal auditing functions.

When an independent auditor decides that the work performed by internal auditors may have a bearing on the nature, extent, and timing of the independent auditor's procedures, the independent auditor should evaluate the competence and objectivity of the internal auditors and review their work as necessary. Relative to objectivity, the independent auditor should consider the organizational level to which internal auditors report the results of their work. To provide the greatest degree of independence in performing internal auditing functions, an internal auditor should report to the board of directors.

Auditor Independence

The auditor ought to retain an attitude characterized by impartiality and fairness towards his clients and anyone who relies on the audit report. This aids the primary purpose of the auditor, to give assurance to the public of the reliability of the company's own reports. The auditor ought to retain independence both in fact and in appearance.

Auditors of publicly owned companies (also known as "issuers") are obligated to disclose any relationships the auditor has with the client company which would have significant bearing on the auditor's independence. The auditor must also confirm his independence in writing, following federal securities statutes and discuss his independence with those charged with governance in the client company.

Functions of the Audit Committee

An **audit committee** is formed by a company's board of directors for the purpose of supervising the audit operation in a company. The audit committee will select and evaluate the CPA firm. According to the SEC, it is mandatory that the audit committee be composed of outside individuals. The audit committee typically reports to the board of directors and shareholders.

The audit committee must review the work of the auditor for quality and scope. It also ensures that auditor recommendations are handled appropriately.

The auditor must communicate with the audit committee, either in writing or orally, the auditor's GAAS responsibility, important accounting policies, accounting estimates, audit adjustments, the auditor's determination of the quality of the client's accounting principles, any disagreements with management, and any challenges encountered in performing the audit. The auditor should document these communications in the audit workpapers.

Importance of Consistency in Financial Reporting

The objective of the reporting standard relating to **consistency** is to give assurance that comparability of financial statements between periods has not been materially affected by changes in accounting principles without disclosure. It is acceptable for a client to use varying accounting principles for differing sections of an account; for example, different methods of depreciation may be used for different asset types. Should an auditor disagree with the client on an accounting principle change, the auditor should issue a modified or adverse opinion, depending on materiality. An emphasis-of-matter or other-matter paragraph should be included, whether the accounting principle changes are GAAP to non-GAAP, GAAP to GAAP, or non-GAAP to GAAP. In the case of comparative financial statements, including the financial statements of a prior period that were examined by a predecessor auditor, whose report is not presented: if the predecessor auditor's report was other than a standard report, the successor auditor must disclose the reasons for any modification of the predecessor auditor's report.

Examples of consideration by the consistency reporting standard:

- A change in the specific subsidiaries that comprise the group of companies for which consolidated statements are presented
- A change from an accounting principle that is not generally accepted to one that is generally accepted
- The correction of a mistake in the application of a change in GAAP.

COMPARATIVE FINANCIAL STATEMENTS

Comparative financial statements are financial statements representing more than one accounting period. The audit report (which must be dated at the last day of fieldwork for the most recent audit) must cover all accounting periods represented. When comparative reports are not retroactively stated, an additional paragraph should be included as long as the year of change is included. When comparative reports are retroactively stated, the additional paragraph need only be included during the year of change.

When dealing with comparative financial statements, there are two primary cases that may cause an unmodified report with explanatory language: 1. If the predecessor auditor has reviewed the prior period financial statements, whether or not to issue the predecessor's audit report must be determined. If it is decided that the report will not be reissued, the successor auditor's report should state the following in the introductory paragraph: the date of the predecessor's audit report, the predecessor's report type, that the prior period financial statements were reviewed by other auditors, and the reasoning for the opinion, if it was not an unmodified standard opinion. 2. If an updated report has a differing opinion from the prior period's opinion, the auditor should state all differing opinion reasons in an explanatory paragraph before the opinion paragraph.

COMMUNICATION WITH THOSE CHARGED WITH GOVERNANCE

There are a number of matters which the auditor ought to discuss with those charged with governance (that is, those with the ultimate responsibility for the organization, including financial reporting). These include the auditor's responsibilities to the company under generally accepted auditing standards (GAAS), such as the auditor's obligation to remain independent and to offer an opinion of the organization's financial statement's accuracy (although the auditor's obligations do not absolve the obligations of management). The auditor also should communicate an overview of his planned audit, yet without making the audit too predictable. Throughout the auditing process, as well, the auditor should inform those charged with governance of any substantial findings he makes concerning errors or fraudulent activity within the company. The auditor should document anything that he communicates to those charged with governance.

Prior to Accepting an Engagement

The auditor must ensure with management, and require as a condition of accepting the engagement, that they assume responsibility both for (1) their financial statements' accordance with the applicable reporting framework (e.g. IFRS or GAAP) – including their decision that such a framework is appropriate for users in their circumstances – and for (2) the *design*, *implementation*, and *maintenance* of their entity's internal controls over financial reporting.

Understanding the Entity and Its Environment

Determination of Materiality Levels for a Financial Statement

It is important for auditors to determine levels of materiality for financial statements taken as a whole, since doing so permits the auditor to calculate the risk of material misstatement and better formulate specific audit procedures for further testing.

Any determination of materiality will be a matter of professional judgment, but some guidelines are instructive. The auditor should choose some financial item (such as revenues, gross profits, net assets) and determine an appropriate benchmark. This could depend on what items are usually depended upon by users of the financial statements and the nature and size of the company and industry. Then, to determine materiality, the auditor should consider various data related to that benchmark and the company as a whole, such as past, present, and future financial results and any special circumstances for the company, such as a merger or an event in the industry as a whole.

Risk Assessment Discussions

It is imperative that the audit team assemble to discuss matters of risk assessment, since it is so easy for various segments of an organization to slip through the cracks and fail to be audited, and also since so many features of the audit are interconnected. Moreover, these discussions allow the more experienced audit team members to disclose advice they may have, and they allow team members to better identify areas of risk within the organization being audited.

Professional Skepticism

Auditors should always plan audits with an attitude of **professional skepticism**, an attitude that includes a questioning mind and critical assessment of audit evidence. Because an audit conducted in accordance with GAAS is influenced by the possibility of material errors, the auditor should conduct the audit with an attitude of professional skepticism.

Examples demonstrating the application of professional skepticism in response to the auditor's assessment of the risk of material misstatement due to fraud include:

- increased sensitivity in the selection of the nature and extent of documentation to be examined in support of material transactions, and
- increased recognition of the need to corroborate management explanations or representations concerning material matters, such as further analytical procedures, the examination of documentation, or discussion with others within or outside the entity.

Errors, Fraud, Illegal Acts, and Defalcation

Errors can be caused by inaccurate measurement, mathematical mistake, or misrepresentation and are generally unintentional. Internal controls can be helpful in limiting the existence of errors. Irregularities are similar to errors, except that irregularities are intentional.

Fraud is an illegal act characterized by intentional deception and often shown by an array of irregularities. In general, material irregularities perpetrated by the controller are the most difficult to detect in the audit.

Illegal acts are violations of laws and governmental regulations.

Defalcation is the actual theft of assets, an example of the misappropriation of assets.

Characteristics of Fraud

Fraud always needs to be duly distinguished by auditors from innocent error. Fraud is an intentional action which results in some particular misstatement, ordinarily for the benefit of the one committing fraud.

Instances of fraud can be split into two categories, financial reporting fraud and the reallocation of assets. The first ("cooking the books") is usually done for the benefit of upper-level management whose pay is partially incentivized by financial results. The second is the direct transfer of money or property to the thieving fraudster.

The causes of fraud can be presented as part of a "fraud triangle," which the three sides signifying pressure, opportunity, and rationalization. **Pressure** consists of a (subjective) incentive to commit fraud, such as the need to have financial statements look good, or perhaps if an employee is struggling to make ends meet. **Opportunity** consists of an objective set of circumstances, such as a failure to segregate duties, which provide an opening for fraud to occur. **Rationalization** consists of the process by which the fraudster justifies the action in his mind, believing perhaps that "he deserves it" or that the company has wronged him.

Risk of Fraud

The audit team ought to get together and brainstorm if there is any issue or risk of material misstatement due to fraud. Such discussion would include areas of the financial statement which could be vulnerable to fraud, what incentives and opportunities management would have to commit fraud (such as the management's ability to override controls), and how assets owned by the company could be stolen. The audit team should then plan controls accordingly, given the risks of fraud.

This communication should occur throughout the audit and should entirely be documented.

Fraud Management

When inquiring of management into the issue of possible fraud in the organization, the auditor should learn several things: whether management is aware or suspicious of any fraud (or allegations of fraud) that impinges on the company, whether management has any insight to provide on areas of fraud risk within the company, including fraud-prevention controls or programs, whether management appropriately conveys the importance of ethics and integrity to other workers, and whether there is proper monitoring for organizations existing in separate locations.

Risk Assessment

Material Misstatements

When assessing the risk of material misstatement due to fraud, the auditor should primarily be looking for any of the three components of the "fraud triangle": pressure, opportunity, and rationalization.

- Examples of pressure would be the declining performance of the company, especially in response to tight competition, high expectations for management to meet certain financial (or other) results, and a high proportion of upper-level executives' salaries being incentivized by financial results.

- Examples of opportunities can include substantial related-party transactions which have gone unaudited, financial statement items which depend upon management estimates, unusual and complicated transactions, and business activity in foreign countries or otherwise significantly dissimilar business environments.
- Examples of rationalization can be based upon a lack of communication concerning the company's expected standards of ethics (thus permitting workers to think they don't *really* apply for them), a large interest by management in improving the company's performance in the stock market (where fraud could be masked as a means to help stockholders), and the involvement of nonfinancial management in financial estimations (where their inaccurate guesses could be excused).

ANALYTICAL PROCEDURES

Analytical procedures seek to identify relationships among sets of financial or nonfinancial data. The effectiveness of the procedures depends not only upon the technology available to the auditor but also upon his knowledge of the business and industry, so that the data exist within a more helpful framework. The purposes of these procedures include helping the auditor as he plans various substantive tests for the organization and helping to provide a final review of the financial data for the organization. Both of these purposes are required according to GAAS. Analytical procedures also can be components of the substantive tests themselves, though that is not required by GAAS.

OBSERVATION AND INSPECTION

Observation and inspection, as simple as they are, can greatly aid an audit process. Different processes for observation and inspection can include reading corporate minutes for meetings of management and those charged with governance, examining the organization's ordinary operations, seeing different records for the business, such as a statement of business strategy or a manual for internal controls, perusing various reports prepared by management or those charged with governance, reading internal audit reports, observing the different places of operation for the organization, and going through the process by which different information is moved through the organization.

INDUSTRY, REGULATORY, AND OTHER FACTORS

Industry, regulatory, and other external factors help to provide an auditor with a wider framework in which to understand the operations and processes of the entity being audited. Industry factors can include all the information which auditors can find concerning competitors ("horizontal") and suppliers and customers ("vertical"), in addition to advances in technology within the industry. Regulatory factors include all the bodies which provide legislative oversight over accounting firms and the firm being audited, such as environmental regulations. And other factors include everything else, such as the general state of the economy.

STRATEGIES AND BUSINESS RISKS

Businesses formulate **strategies** to achieve objectives which are designed in response to various factors (internal and external) related to the business. **Business risks** are those events or states of affairs which could prohibit a business from fulfilling its objectives as desired. And even though it is not true that all business risks provide a risk of material misstatement, they nonetheless have some bearing upon the financial statement.

Auditors are not required to learn of all the business risks for the firm being audited, though they should inquire of management as to their method of responding to and addressing business risks.

Financial Performance Measures

In reviewing the company's financial performance, and especially its performance measures, the auditor can learn of the company as it is and as it aims to be, which can provide possible motivation for management to misstate different items. Performance measures also indicate which elements of the company management deems important, which can provide guidance to the auditor for his own audit procedures.

Financial performance measures can be internal (such as reports on the performance of particular departments, variance reports, and budgets) or external (such as reports done by business analysts or credit agencies).

Control Risk

Control risk is the risk that the client's internal control system will fail to detect material misstatements. Control risk should not be assessed so low that complete reliance is on controls and no other audit work is performed. Conversely, setting it at 100% is a possibility, and it essentially means that no reliance is on controls. The relationship between control risk and substantive evidence is direct (high control risk = more substantive evidence). During the planning stages of the audit, the auditor will document his understanding of internal control. At this point, the auditor will determine his planned assessed level of control risk for the financial statement assertions. There are cases in which the auditor will perform additional tests of controls once this assessed level of control risk has been determined during the planning stages:

- The auditor thinks that the controls are effective and has evidence to support this, causing control risk to be below the maximum level.
- The auditor thinks that the controls are ineffective, which would cause the maximum level of control risk.
- The auditor thinks that the controls are effective, but the cost of testing them is too great; in this scenario, control risk is at the maximum level. When there is no evidence supporting the auditor's assessment, control risk is assessed at the maximum level.

Internal Controls

Internal controls are processes within an organization designed to provide reasonable assurance regarding (1) the reliability and integrity of financial reporting (which is most relevant to the audit), (2) compliance of the firm with policies, plans, procedures, laws, and regulations, (3) the safeguarding of assets, (4) the economical and efficient use of resources, (5) the accomplishment of established objectives and goals for operations or programs, and (6) the effectiveness and efficiency of operations.

It is important for the auditor to understand the client's internal controls to locate any potential material misstatements, to be aware of any issues that would affect the risk of material misstatements, and to conduct effective substantive tests. Since the auditor will report on the sufficiency of existing controls within a company, the auditor will consider internal controls to plan the audit. Control test work is often conducted at interim periods during the year and updated during the year-end test work. Controls are tested to determine the control operation or the design's effectiveness. Two opinions are included on internal control: whether management's assessment is fairly stated, and whether the company maintained effective internal control over financial reporting.

Internal Control and the Control Hierarchy

Internal control is the use of control plans to achieve control goals in operations systems and information systems. Internal control is the responsibility of management. Internal control is needed to improve the possibility that results will be achieved, to help the organization meet its objectives, to protect the organization's resources, to ensure the organization produces reliable financial statements, and to ensure the organization (management) meets legal responsibilities.

The **control hierarchy** consists of the following levels:

1. **Control environment**: corporate ethics and management integrity, commitment to competence, and organizational structure and culture.
2. **Pervasive controls**: relate to a multitude of goals and applications, are broad in scope and influence the effectiveness of application control plans.
   2a. **General controls**: a subset of pervasive controls; relates only to computer systems; made up of access controls, data controls, hardware and software controls, and operation controls.
3. **Application controls**: specific to the application (focus on transaction processing).
   a. Internal controls do have limitations, such as faulty human judgment, human errors, management's ability to override, and cost restrictions. One method of determining if client's management may have overridden internal control is to review differences disclosed in exception reports.

COSO Framework for Internal Controls

The **Committee of Sponsoring Organizations (COSO)** has a framework for internal control which subdivides internal controls into five components: the control environment, risk assessment, information and communication, control activities, and monitoring. The **control environment** is the most fundamental component and consists of the "culture" and mindset of the company; it is especially influenced by the mindset and behavior of management. **Risk assessment** consists of the identification of and significance attributed to various business risks. **Information and communication** involves the transfer of information within the organization, especially the efficiency of information transfer. **Control activities** consist of those policies which influence and enforce compliance with the objectives and messages of management. And **monitoring** involves the periodic assessment of internal controls, testing their effectiveness and seeking improvement.

Business Processes and Information Flows

The primary concern for the auditor in understanding business processes and information flows is to be comprehensive, to avoid missing relevant details. This requires him to keep in mind the various elements of internal control (for instance, according to COSO's five categories) and to have a map of information sources, as well as a record of risk assessment procedures already performed.

Whenever there is any discussion the auditor has concerning the risk of material misstatement, whether due to unintentional error or due to fraud, the auditor should document all details of the discussion, such as the manner, location, content, parties, and results of it.

Information Technology

Information technology helps to improve the effectiveness and efficiency of a company's internal controls by automating the controls process and the monitoring of it. Information technology makes certain information confidential and can require other people's permission to engage in various processes, thus facilitating an appropriate segregation of duties. It also provides much aid in the rapid transfer of information through the entity.

Computer Controls

Computer controls are internal controls performed by computer software controls as opposed to manual controls, and also refers to general and application controls over the computer processing of data. Computer controls should be tested by auditors, and application controls can be tested through reperformance. General application controls can be tested by using observation and inquiry. Programmed controls consist of input controls and processing controls. Computer systems use either batch processing periodically, or online real-time processing.

- Auditors should bear in mind that internal control computer systems can possibly end up in transaction trails that either are only in computer-readable form or exist for a short time period.
- Internal control computer systems can possibly contain program errors that would cause transactions to be processed incorrectly. At the same time, human errors can occur less frequently when using computer systems.
- Computer-driven internal control systems can cause less supporting documentation due to the computer's handling of information.
- The same rules apply for control risk in computer systems for internal control purposes. For example, the auditor will test the operating effectiveness if the control risk is assessed below the maximum.

Risk Assessment Procedures

The different risk assessment procedures performed by the auditor for the client company depend upon a number of factors, but the types of risk assessment procedures can nevertheless be split into several different categories. The auditor can make **inquiries**, usually of management and whoever else is responsible for the company's financial reporting, but also of other workers, like the internal audit team. The auditor can also engage in **analytics** in an attempt to discern any relationships with subsist among the firm's data, and participate in **observation and inspection** of different aspects of the firm. He can obtain **prior period information**, using past information to appropriately gauge the present risk of material misstatement for different elements of the firm. And he can also do specific tests for **fraud risk**, finding the risk of material misstatement due to such intentional violations.

General Controls in a Financial IT Environment Risks

One of the drawbacks of widespread automation is the possibility of devastation whenever some widespread problem occurs. Thus it is crucial that firms have an appropriate backup plan for their information technology systems, especially for their financial IT.

Another drawback of widespread automation is the fact that relatively few people—those who have the most knowledge of how the system works and how it can be overridden—have the most power over it. This makes it especially crucial for companies to have appropriate segregation of duties with respect to financial IT, including dispensing limited network access and administrative rights.

Application Functionality for Financial Transaction Cycles Risks

An auditor needs to be concerned with the chance of error involved with the use of automated processes for inputting financial transactions. It is especially easy for the functionality of new applications to give way to errors in the process as users become accustomed to the new programs. There also can be an increased risk of material misstatement arising from the integration of different applications and the complexity of e-commerce, as well as significant or complex algorithms involved in these applications. It is vital for the auditor to be aware of all of these potential errors.

Internal Controls for Reliable Financial Reporting

Internal controls for reliable financial reporting give the auditor something to rely on and reduce the need for him to perform substantive tests on the results of different financial transactions. This is because they are designed to ensure that financial records accurately reflect the amount and nature of transactions, that financial reports are prepared according to the applicable reporting framework (e.g. GAAP), that purchases and expenditures are appropriately authorized according the company's hierarchy, and that any unauthorized use of assets is caught within a reasonable amount of time.

It is particularly important that an auditor pay special attention to period-end financial reporting, since that time period serves as an opportunity for management to sneak in inappropriate transactions (such as some related-party transactions) or inappropriate representations of transactions (such as understating expenses).

Limitations of Internal Control

The first limitation of internal control is that it can provide merely reasonable assurance, not absolute assurance, that the firm's objectives are being fulfilled. The degree of assurance, as a benefit, needs to be weighed against the costs of implementing and monitoring the processes comprising the company's internal controls. Another drawback of internal control is that it is merely *internal*; it can aid in the accomplishment of the company's objectives, but it necessarily will be unable to address the numerous external factors which can inhibit the fulfillment of such objectives.

Service Organizations

Service organizations simply provide various services to user organizations, one example of which would be a credit-processing organization which facilitates the user organization's transactions. Service organizations are relevant to the auditor because of their impact on the control environment of the client firm. Service auditors report on the activity of the service organization in processing transactions, whereas user auditors evaluate the reliability of the user organization's financial reports.

Statement on Auditing Standards (SAS) 70 and AT 801 provide additional guidance to auditors for their interaction with service organizations.

Management Override

Since firms rarely want to be in a position where even their own management cannot make exceptions to policies for the good of the company, management is sometimes given the capacity to override various controls that are in place. But an obvious risk is that this power can be used to facilitate fraud, so much so that most companies outright prohibit it. Consequently, it is imperative that auditors not simply rely on the nature of the internal controls in order to determine the amount and nature and subsequent substantive testing. Instead, auditors should also ensure that there is appropriate compliance with internal controls, especially by upper-level management, who might have incentives to alter financial reports.

Nature and Causes of Misstatements

Misstatements can be either known or likely, with the uncertainty of (merely) likely misstatements arising either from disagreements with managements concerning the application of some accounting principle or estimate, or from an auditor's projection of the error rate for a sample population to the whole.

Misstatements can be caused by unintentional error or by fraud. And although the auditor should not be concerned with immaterial misstatements caused by unintentional error, he still should be concerned with any evidence (whether material or immaterial) for fraud, since that could signify a larger problem.

Financial Statement Assertions

Financial statement assertions can consist of any statement whatsoever that signifies the financial condition of the company or transactional events in which it participated. For transactions, auditors should test for their occurrence, completeness, accuracy, and classification, in addition to ensuring that the transaction process was appropriately authorized and completed before the cutoff period. For accounts balances, auditors should test for their existence and completeness and should ensure that the balances are valued properly.

Audit objectives, in a broad sense, include the auditor's goals to assess internal controls and ensure compliance with them, to substantively test different accounts, to discern the risk of error, and to provide an audit opinion. An auditor should be able to provide more flesh to these objectives, making them more specific for the client company, as he learns more about its particular processes and reports.

Material Misstatement on the Financial Statements

It is easy to distinguish between material and immaterial errors or risks of misstatement as those which are significant or meaningful versus those which are not, but it is more difficult to specifically quantify the threshold for materiality for particular transactions. Part of this difficulty stems from the different contexts in which different errors can be material, as well as from the fact that certain material errors are not quantitative (e.g. failing to disclose a particular related-party transaction). Consequently, a quantitative criterion of materiality cannot be provided for firms universally, but must always be specified to the particular characteristics of a firm, including its nature and size, and its industry.

Risk of Material Misstatement Assessment

The auditor is obligated to assess the risk of material misstatement for financial statement level assertions and specific assertions. Some errors can have pervasive effects on the financial statements (and ordinarily are traceable to specific assertions), while other risks can be formulated merely in terms of their effects on particular accounts. Some financial statement level risks exist without a clear relation to specific assertions, such as the risk of an unethical company environment. It is important for all of these that the auditor correctly judge risk as it exists at these different levels.

Relevance of Recent Economic, Accounting, or Other Developments

The auditor must be aware of various external developments when performing an audit, since a number of things can impinge on the audit. A downturn in the economy, with its concomitant decrease of customer demand, could put additional pressure on management to put out good financial results through fraudulent misstatement of financial items. Alternatively, changes in accounting standards can modify the pattern to which clients ought to conform in their processes and accounts.

Related Parties and Related-Party Transactions

Companies ought to report related-party transactions in accordance with the reporting framework, which involves an emphasis upon the economic substance (as opposed to legal form) of the transaction, including loans, sales, and free services between or among parents and subsidiaries.

The auditor should be aware not only of the transactions themselves but of conditions in which such transactions are more likely to occur, understanding that businesses are sometimes designed to deliberately conceal related-party transactions. Such conditions could include pressure for an improved earnings record, a substantial amount of litigation, and a chance of obsolescence due to technological development (in which case obsolete things might be dumped to a subsidiary).

The auditor should also believe that related-party transactions are independent of the business's ordinary operations only if he has good evidence to do so.

Improper Revenue Recognition

One of the ways in which a company can depart from the reporting framework standards (e.g. GAAP) is through improper revenue recognition. This can be done through channel stuffing (deliberately selling more than a retailer can accept in order to inflate accounts receivable for a given period), shipping unfinished products, unduly liberal return or exchange policies, fictitious transactions, and other ways.

An auditor also ought to be aware of nonroutine or complex transactions, since such transactions might be concealing activity which does not comply with the reporting framework.

Significant Management Estimates

Many account balances rely on management estimates, usually because they are based on future contingencies. These accounts can include warranty liabilities, allowances for doubtful accounts, pension liabilities, evaluations of fixed assets, and assessments of goodwill. Such management estimates are unavoidable, but it is vital that the auditor ensure that these estimates, the significant estimates in particular, be based upon solid, objective, and independent evidence—not mere hunches. Estimates often give grounds for management to unduly inflate performance measures for the firm, making it important for auditors to keep an eye on significant management estimates.

Illegal Acts

Other than failures to conform to the reporting framework, it is obvious that auditors should be aware of possible illegal activity in the client company. This can include the violation of tax laws, collusion with other firms, and bribing domestic or foreign officials. Consequently, the auditor's procedures should be designed to detect illegal activity if it exists; this might involve perusing corporate minutes and being suspicious of large payments to unspecified customers or to the government.

If the auditor discovers an illegal act, or an apparently illegal act, then he should consult with the client's legal expert to ensure that the acts are indeed illegal. The auditor also ought to disclose the illegal activity to the board of directors' audit committee and sometimes to the SEC.

Performing Audit Procedures and Evaluating Evidence

Risks of Material Misstatement

Responses

Beyond and prior to the implementation of particular audit procedures to detect material misstatements, an auditor can employ some overall responses to risks of material misstatement. These can include a discussion with one's audit committee to reinforce the importance of professional skepticism or the request of specialists or otherwise more experienced staff members to carry out the audit. These can also include overall changes to the nature, timing, and extent of types of audit procedures.

Nature, Extent, and Timing of Other Audit Procedures

According to SAS 110, the audit procedures can vary according to their nature, being either procedural or substantive, and they can vary according to their type, being concerned with observation, inspection, inquiry, analytics, and others.

The extent of audit procedures depends on the auditor's determination of the level of tolerable misstatement, the risk of material misstatement, and the desired degree of assurance that the statements are free of error. Audit procedures can sometimes be extended with the help of computer technology.

Part of the timing of audit procedures involves whether to perform them at the end of a period or at some interim date. An increased risk of material misstatement should influence an auditor to perform more substantive tests at period-end, or even to execute his auditing procedures at unexpected times.

Address Assessing Risks

Whenever an auditor encounters something he has assessed to be a risk for material misstatement, he should appropriately document his identification of it. This includes all the details concerning the department for it, the workers possibly responsible for it, and any interaction with workers or (especially) with management concerning steps to correct any deficiencies.

The auditor also ought to evaluate controls related to the risks in order to determine if the risk is symptomatic of larger control issues.

Level of Tolerable Misstatement

The **level of tolerable misstatement** is the maximal degree to which a particular account may be misstated such that, when combined with other misstatements, the financial reports are still materially accurate. In other words, it is the maximum degree of misstatement which an auditor can deem immaterial. The level of tolerable misstatement will necessarily be, to some extent, a judgment call by the auditor.

Increases in tolerable misstatements allow for less substantive testing and smaller sample sizes.

TYPES OF EVIDENCE

Types of Evidence:

1. **Physical examination** – the inspection of a tangible asset, determining wheter the asset exists
2. **Confirmation** – a written or oral response from a third party
3. **External documentation** – the examination of a client's documents and records when the document is from outside the client's organization (vouching)
4. **Reperformance** – rechecking computations or transfers of information (tracing)
5. **Internal documentation** (good internal control) – the examination of the client's documents and records when the document is prepared and used within the client's organization (vouching)
6. **Observation** – directly observing an activity or facility
7. **Analytical procedures** – making comparisons to judge reasonableness
8. **Internal documentation** (weak internal control) – the examination of the client's internal documents and records
9. **Inquiries of client** – asking questions (oral or written response) of the client

AUDITING PROCEDURES

Auditing procedures are tasks the auditor undertakes for collecting, analyzing, interpreting, and documenting information during an audit. Audit procedures are the means to attain audit objectives. They differ from auditing standards, in that procedures relate to acts to be performed.

- Audit procedures include: **analytical procedures** (where balances are reviewed to identify significant fluctuations and relationships between balances), inspection (scrutinizing or critically examining a document), **inquiry** (asking questions of client personnel), **observation** (watching and testing a client action, such as taking inventory), and **confirmation** (communication with outside parties to authenticate internal evidence).
- An **audit program** lists the audit procedures to be followed during an audit. The audit program also states the objectives of the audit. Instructions in an audit program include various terms, such as:
    - agree – match balances
    - foot – total a column, or group of numbers
    - read
    - reconcile (reconciliation) – involves a schedule establishing agreement between separate sources of information, such as accounting records reconciled with the financial statements

INTEGRATED AUDITS

Integrated audits are combinations of audits over financial statements and audits of internal control over financial reporting (ICOFR). The goal for auditors who are performing integrated audits is to efficiently and effectively implement tests which provide procedural and substantive assessments to ensure the reliability of financial statements and of ICOFR.

ASSESSING DESIGN EFFECTIVENESS

Auditors should ensure that the internal controls for the client company are both designed effectively and operating effectively. The **design effectiveness** of a set of controls refers to its aim to either prevent or detect material errors within a reasonable amount of time. When evaluating a set of control's design effectiveness, auditors ought to look for missing controls (which therefore cannot even be tested for design in the first place), such as monitoring controls and governance controls, a failure of controls to meet their control objectives, and the concentration of duties with a single person when they are incompatible or otherwise ought to be segregated,

Monitoring Component of Internal Control

Monitoring is how management periodically assesses the quality of internal control performance. The monitoring activities often include the audit of the annual financial statements.

When understanding and documenting test of controls, the auditor should engage in various audit procedures, such as updating workpapers, making inquiries, reading manuals, examining documents, and observing. These procedures and their resulting documentation apply to all five components of the internal control structure for both design and operation.

An auditor's documentation of tests of control should involve a narrative, a flowchart, and internal control questionnaires. The auditor will often use a flowchart to document his understanding of internal control. The independent auditor should acquire an understanding of the internal audit function as it relates to the independent auditor's consideration of the internal control, because the work performed by internal auditors may be a factor in determining the nature, timing, and extent of the independent auditor's procedures. The auditor's understanding of the client's internal control is documented in order to substantiate compliance with generally accepted auditing standards.

Assessing Operating Effectiveness

Auditors should ensure that the internal controls for the client company are both designed effectively and operating effectively. The **operating effectiveness** of a set of controls refers to its ability to fulfill its design of preventing and detecting material errors. An auditor should test controls' operating effectiveness only for controls which he expects to be able to prevent or detect material misstatements in a timely manner.

Examples of tests for operating effectiveness can include inquiring of management or employees, inspecting relevant documents and files, observing the control as it is employed, and reperforming the control.

Substantive Procedures

Substantive procedures seek to identify material misstatements at the assertion level, trying to find errors in the substance of the accounts themselves. Different types of substantive procedures test for different elements of an account, such as its existence, completeness, rights and obligations, valuation and allocation, and presentation and disclosure. Substantive tests can also include analytical procedures. The auditor ought to plan substantive testing so as to respond to the planned level of detection risk for the audit.

Sampling

Sampling involves applying an audit procedure to less than 100% of the population. Sampling can be divided into four steps: plan, select, perform, and evaluate.

Advantages of using statistical sampling include the following:

1. Statistical sampling aids in the design of an efficient sample.
2. Statistical sampling allows the auditor to measure the sufficiency of the evidential matter obtained.
3. Statistical sampling provides a means for mathematically measuring the degree of risk that results from examining only part of a population.

a. The application of statistical sampling techniques is related to the three standards of fieldwork.
b. When using statistical sampling for tests of controls, an auditor's evaluation process would include a statistical conclusion about whether procedural deviation in the population was within an acceptable range.

Audit Sampling Terminology

The **tolerable misstatement** is the amount of misstatement the auditor will permit in the population before action is required (essentially a preliminary judgment about materiality). It is given as a percent.

The **acceptable risk of incorrect acceptance** is the risk that the sample supports the conclusion that the recorded account balance is not materially misstated when it is materially misstated. It is given as a percent. The risk of incorrect acceptance and the risk of assessing control risk too low relate to the effectiveness of the audit.

The **population exception rate** is used when determining sample size. It is an estimate of misstatement in a population and given as a percent.

Misstatement bounds are the results, the estimates of the likely maximum overstatement and likely maximum understatement.

The **tolerable error**, in variable sampling, is the greatest misstatement amount the auditor believes can exist in a balance or transactions class without resulting in a material misstatement of the financial statements.

Steps Involved in Attribute Sampling

Steps for attribute sampling and determining sample size.

Planning

1. Set objective. Example: existence
2. Define attribute and exception. Example: shipping document not attached to sales invoice
3. Define population. Example: sales invoices for year
4. Define sampling unit. Example: a sales invoice
5. Specify tolerable exception rate. Example: 6% (judgment)
6. Specify acceptable risk of assessing control risk too low. Example: 5% (judgment)
7. Estimate population exception rate. Example: 2% (judgment, past experience)
8. Determine initial sample size. Example: 127

Select the Sample

9. Select the sample. Example: invoice #'s 3689, 4150, etc.

Perform the Tests

10. Perform the test.

Attribute Sampling

Attribute sampling is a statistical procedure used to study the characteristics of a population, the audit sampling which is used for tests of controls and substantive tests of transactions.

1. Attribute sampling is qualitative in nature.
2. The goal is to estimate the proportion of items in a population (the exception rate) containing an attribute of interest. With tests of controls, the auditor is interested in deviations from client's established controls; with tests of transactions, the auditor is interested in monetary errors or irregularities in populations of transaction data.
3. When performing tests of controls, attribute sampling is the most useful.
4. An auditor examining inventory may appropriately apply sampling for attributes in order to estimate the percentage of slow-moving inventory items.
5. A 10% change in the population size would not have much of an effect on the statistical sample.
6. If all other factors specified in an attribute sampling plan remain constant, changing the specified tolerable deviation rate from 6% to 10%, and changing the specified risk from 97% to 93%, would cause the required sample size to decrease.
7. In estimation sampling for attributes, the sample size must be known in order to appraise the results of the auditor's sample.

Non-Sampling Risk, Non-Sampling Errors, and Sampling Errors

Nonsampling risk is any audit risk which is not due to sampling. An auditor may apply a procedure to all transactions or balances and fail to detect a material misstatement.

Nonsampling risk includes the possibility of selecting audit procedures that are not appropriate to achieve a specific objective. For example, confirming recorded receivables cannot reveal unrecorded receivables. Nonsampling risk can be reduced to a negligible level through adequate planning and supervision.

Examples of nonsampling risk include:

1. Failing to evaluate results properly.
2. Use of an audit procedure inappropriate to achieve a given audit objective.
3. Failure to recognize an error.

Nonsampling error is the auditor's failure to recognize a misstatement in an amount or a deviation in an internal control, data-processing procedure.

Sampling error is the difference between the sampling value and the population value (if it had been tested).

Statistical and Nonstatistical Sampling

Both nonstatistical and statistical methodologies are acceptable under current audit guidelines (though in most settings, statistical is preferred).

Statistical means being able to quantify sampling risk in planning and evaluating audit testing.

Nonstatistical (or judgmental) means relying on professional judgment to select items and evaluate. An example of nonstatistical sampling would be haphazard sampling.

Statistical sampling refers to tests of controls where the population size has little to no effect on determining sample size except for very small populations.

Sampling risks is the possibility that conclusions drawn from the sample may not represent correct conclusions for the entire population; a randomly chosen sample may not be representative of the population as a whole.

One element of sampling risk is choosing a sample size that is too small to achieve the sampling objective.

In assessing sampling risk, the risk of incorrect rejection and the risk of assessing control risk too high relate to the efficiency of the audit.

STATISTICAL SELECTION TECHNIQUES

There are certain statistical selection techniques that are desirable for use by auditors. **Systematic** selection may be appropriate if certain forms are not consecutively numbered. For example, in examining cash disbursements, an auditor plans to choose a sample using systematic selection with a random start. The primary advantage is that population items do not have to be pre-numbered for the auditor to use the technique. **Stratified** selection is used to select a greater percentage of accounts with high balances than accounts with low balances. For example, if an auditor was reviewing cash disbursements and there were a few unusually large disbursements, the CPA's best course of action is to stratify the cash disbursements population so large disbursements are reviewed separately. **Sequential** selection doesn't use a fixed sample size for tests of controls. **Discovery sampling** is exploratory sampling to assure that the proportion of units with a particular attribute isn't in excess of a given percentage of the population; it uses the population size, minimum unacceptable error rate, and confidence level. If the auditor is concerned that a population may contain exceptions, the determination of a sample size sufficient to include at least one such exception is a characteristic of discovery sampling. Discovery sampling shouldn't be used if a CPA estimates that the occurrence rate of a certain characteristic in a population being examined exceeds approximately 0%.

REPRESENTATIONAL SAMPLING

Auditors hope to perform audit procedures on a **representational sample**, i.e., where the audit characteristics of the sample is approximately the same as the population. However, regardless of sampling methodology, there is a **sampling risk** that the sample is **not** representative. Hence, sample selection methods are important. Sample selection methods include:

Judgmental sampling: using the auditor's professional judgment

- Directed: picking ones that might have the most errors
- Block: items in a sequence
- Haphazard: anything goes

Probabilistic sampling: statistical-based

- Random number: uses a random number table or computer program and establishes correspondence between the table and the population item of interest, to select items. An underlying feature of the random-based selection of items is that each item in the accounting population should have an opportunity to be selected.

Systematic: every 20th item, etc. This can be biased.

Probability-proportional to size (PPS) and **stratified**: used in monetary unit sampling and variables sampling ($ value).

Sample Size

↑ Estimated Population Exception Rate; ↑ Sample Size

Look at this from the perspective of precision. Precision is equal to the tolerable exception rate minus the estimated population exception rate. The smaller the number from this calculation, the more precise the auditors are trying to be, and the greater the sample needs to be. In comparison to what the auditors set the tolerable exception rate at, a less precise estimate will be required with a low estimated population exception rate (the estimated population exception rate will be further away from tolerable exception rate), so a relatively small sample will satisfy the auditor's tolerable exception rate. In sum, to be more precise (a relatively higher estimated population exception rate, closer to tolerable exception rate), auditors need more data and thus a larger sample.

↑ Population; ↑ Sample size (minor increase)

If the sample is representative, population size is a minor consideration. The tables are based on "infinitely" large quantities, so if the auditor is looking at a very small population, he may use a finite correction factor. The sample size has an inverse relationship with tolerable misstatements and the desired risk of incorrect acceptance and incorrect rejection. The sample size has a direct relationship with the misstatements' expected size and frequency.

Various Aspects of Sampling

Risk of assessing too low, unrestricted random sampling, deviations in samples, risk of assessing too high, and the risk of assessing control risk too low in various population sizes.

The risk that the assessed level of control risk based on the sample is less than the true operating effectiveness of the control structure policy or procedure is termed **the risk of assessing too low**.

Suppose an auditor initially planned to use **unrestricted random sampling** with replacement in the examination of accounts receivable. Later, the auditor decided to use unrestricted random sampling without replacement. As a result only of this decision, the sample size should decrease.

Suppose an auditor plans to examine a sample of 20 checks for countersignatures as prescribed by the client's internal control procedures. One of the checks in the chosen sample of 20 cannot be found. The auditor should consider the reasons for this limitation and treat the missing check as a **deviation** when evaluating the sample.

The risk that the assessed level of control risk based on the sample is greater than the true operating effectiveness of the control structure policy or procedure is termed **risk of assessing too high**.

Given random selection, the same sample size, and the same tolerable deviation rate for the testing of two unequal populations, the risk of **assessing control risk too low for the smaller population** is lower than the risk of assessing too low for the larger population.

Determining Sample Size, Assessing the Tolerable Rate, and Factors Affecting the Sample Size

To determine the number of items to be selected in a sample for a particular substantive test of details, the auditor should consider the tolerable misstatement, allowable risk of incorrect acceptance, and characteristics of the population.

The **size** of a sample designed for dual-purpose testing should be the larger of the samples that would otherwise have been designed for the two separate purposes.

When assessing the **tolerable rate**, the auditor should consider that, while deviations from control procedures increase the risk of material errors, such deviations do not necessarily result in errors. This explains why a recorded disbursement that does not show evidence of required approval may nevertheless be a transaction that is properly authorized and recorded.

A number of factors influence the **sample size** for a substantive test of details of an account balance. All other factors being equal, a smaller measure of tolerable misstatements would lead to a larger sample size.

Evaluating the Results in Attribute Sampling

When evaluating the results in attribute sampling, one should do the following:

- Generalize from sample to population. Example: 5% acceptable risk of accepting control risk too low, 127 in sample, 2 exceptions = 5.0 which is the computed upper precision limit
- Analyze exceptions
- Decide acceptability of population
- The auditor is willing to rely on the control (reduce control risk) if the rate of missing documents in the population does not exceed 6% (tolerable exception rate), at a 5% acceptable risk of assessing control risk too low. On the basis of past experience, the estimated population exception rate is 2%. Based on testing, the worst likely exception rate in the population (computed upper precision limit) at this acceptable risk of assessing control risk too low (5%) is 5.0. Since that number is below the tolerable exception rate, the conclusion is that the control being tested can be relied on.

Confirming Balances and Transactions with Third Parties

The confirmation of balances and transactions with independent third parties serves as very persuasive evidence for an audit, whether it be positive or negative. As with other auditing procedures, the auditor should seek out a sample size of third-party transactions and then perform analyses to identify any discrepancies for the transactions in terms of existence, completeness, or any other facet of the transactions.

Inventory Internal Controls and Substantive Procedures

Examples of internal controls for inventory can include the requirement for inventory acquisitions to be approved, the assurance that proper physical controls are in place to protect inventory from theft, and that the recording of inventory is in line with the reporting framework, e.g. GAAP (or that all departures from the framework are justified).

Examples of substantive procedures for inventory can include inventory cost method testing, analytical procedures to verify the reasonableness for inventory balances, and basic calculations, such as inventory turnover rates.

Tests of Details, Tests of Transactions, and Tests of Balances

Tests of details are substantive procedures which are more appropriate for specific assertions that need to be tested, rather than for a large quantity of assertions. They can be subdivided into different categories depending upon what is being tested.

Tests of transactions are tests of details focused on the existence and completeness of a company's transactions according to their own records, Tests of transactions can sometimes be performed at the same time as tests of controls.

Tests of balances specifically seek misstatements in account balances, concerned with specific accounts and not transaction cycles.

COMPUTER-ASSISTED AUDIT TECHNIQUES (CAATS)

Computer-assisted audit techniques (CAATs) seek to increase audit efficiency and effectiveness by providing more automation to the process. The computer tools which are introduced as CAATs can range from the more simple use of word processors, text editing programs, and spreadsheets to more complex tools used for statistical analysis and specialized software. Besides its widespread use for data analysis, CAATs also can be employed to create electronic work papers, to detect fraud, and to continuously monitor compliance with internal controls.

AUDIT PROCEDURES FOR SIGNIFICANT MANAGEMENT ESTIMATES

Sometimes management will have to make accounting estimates, either because the account amount is based on future uncertainties or because the cost of accumulating the relevant data to eliminate uncertainty is very cost-ineffective. Examples of these include net realizable values for inventory, allowance for doubtful accounts, and revenues from contracted accounted for using the percentage-of-completion method.

The auditor is required to test the reasonableness of these management estimates, testing as best as he can the objective and subjective factors involved in their formulation. This includes an analysis of the data utilized by management to reach their conclusions in addition to all their relevant assumptions.

FAIR VALUE MEASUREMENTS

Fair value measurements can occur at the time of an item's acquisition or whenever the item undergoes a change in value. Auditors should seek to identify and evaluate the process which management has authorized for the determination of the fair value of different assets, liabilities, or components of equity. Since fair value, according to Governmental Accounting Standards Board Statement 31, is the price that would be received to transfer some item in an orderly transaction on the date of measurement, the management should have market information and corresponding assumptions to show how such fair values are determined.

UNUSUAL YEAR-END TRANSACTIONS

An easier way to misrepresent financial data is to squeeze in inappropriate transactions which then exit from the books at year-end. Hence, for the auditor, significant and unusual year-end transactions serve as good grounds for him to be suspicious.

Unusual transactions include ones which are unduly complex, especially ones involving related parties, such as subsidiaries. If it seems to the auditor that extra attention was given by management to the form of the communicated data rather than to its economic substance, he should investigate the nature of such transactions further.

INTERNATIONAL STANDARDS ON AUDITING (ISAS)

International Standards on Auditing (ISAs) are issued by the International Auditing and Assurance Standards Board (IAASB) of the International Federation of Accountants (IFAC). Sometimes, auditors practicing within the United States will need to audit a client in compliance with ISAs. In addition to this, these auditors will need to conform to generally accepted auditing standards for nonissuing companies and to the PCAOB's standards for issuing companies.

Auditor's Evaluation of Contingencies

Contingencies pose a problem within audits due to their uncertainty. There are two factors to every contingency: the estimated amount of the contingency and the probability of the relevant event's occurrence. For both of these factors, the auditor should seek to understand and assess the process by which they are calculated and be particularly aware of the possibility of significant contingent liabilities failing to make it onto the company's balance sheet.

Litigation and Lawyers' Letters

It is important that an auditor properly understand the litigation cases and claims in which the client company is involved. This includes understanding the condition or event causing legal action and the degree and probability of potential loss. This information can be obtained through a letter of audit inquiry issued to the client company's lawyer. In the event that the auditor believes legal proceedings could contribute to a material misstatement, he ought to contact the legal counsel directly – rather than requesting management to contact him.

Subsequent Events

Subsequent events are examined during the audit after year-end. There are two categories of subsequent events:

1. Events that give new evidence regarding issues that were in existence as of the balance sheet date. In these events, the financial statements should be adjusted for any applicable estimate changes.
2. Events that give new evidence regarding issues that were not in existence as of the balance sheet date. These events should be disclosed as footnote disclosures.
    a. hould the auditor discover that necessary audit procedures were not performed during the course of the audit prior to issuing an opinion, the importance of the procedures should be evaluated. If the omitted procedures are significant, alternative procedures should be immediately conducted. If the auditor then discovers misstatements, he should examine his obligations on the subsequent discovery of facts that are in existence at the date of the auditor's report. Should the client not permit the auditor to conduct alternative procedures, the auditor should obtain advice from his lawyer.

Management Representations

Generally accepted auditing standards require management to obtain management representations in written form. The purpose of such written representations is to confirm orally communicated management representations and to diminish the chance of misunderstandings in the auditor's interaction with the company. Management representations can help the auditor to complement other audit evidence, although they sometimes give rise to a contradiction, in which case the auditor should perform further investigation.

Inspecting the Entity's Regulatory Compliance

When inspecting the entity's regulatory compliance, the auditor not merely must perform the relevant procedures ensuring compliance, but also must inspect any correspondence between the entity and regulatory authorities to learn possible areas of inspection.

Evaluating Audit Findings, Communications, and Reporting

Conclusion of the Audit Procedures

Audit procedures to be finalized at the conclusion of the audit:

- Complete disclosure checklist
- Conduct subsequent events review
- Complete final analyticals
- Examine minutes from shareholder meetings, board of directors meetings, and audit committee meetings
- Obtain the management representation letter
- Complete the search for unrecorded liabilities
- Assess any audit findings. During the audit, the auditor may propose adjusting journal entries for the client from any material misstatements that come to the auditor's attention during the course of the audit. All material misstatements must be corrected, or an unmodified opinion cannot be issued. At the audit's conclusion, any unrecorded misstatements are combined into the total likely misstatement. The auditor will evaluate this misstatement to determine if any further action should be taken.
- Workpapers need to be reviewed by manager and partners
- Communicate with the audit committee

Overall Analytical Procedures

Overall analytical procedures can aid an auditor by simultaneously offering both substantive and procedural information and giving him a general "map" of how he wishes to engage the rest of the audit. But they are also helpful at the end of the audit, to provide an overall review, providing confirmation or disconfirmation of conclusions reached on the financial statement or on other data. Overall analytic reviews aid the auditor in discerning whether additional testing is necessary and for assessing whether the client company is a going concern.

Sufficient, Reliable Evidence

Evidence (evidential matter) includes written and electronic information (such as checks, records of electronic fund transfers, invoices, contracts, and other information) that permits the auditor to reach conclusions through proper reasoning. Competent evidence needs to be both **relevant** (capable of making a difference in decision making) and **valid** (attesting to the accuracy and reliability of evidence).

Sufficiency is a measure of the quantity of audit evidence. The independent auditor's objective is to obtain sufficient competent evidence to provide a reasonable basis for forming an opinion.

When looking at evidence, consider its **reliability**:

1. Evidence from an independent provider is more reliable than evidence obtained internally within the entity. If the provider is independent, consider the qualifications of the provider to ensure that the evidence should be reliable.

2. The independent auditor's direct personal knowledge, from physical examination, observation, computation, and inspection, is more persuasive than information obtained indirectly.
3. Consider if the client's internal control structure is strong, weak or somewhere in the middle. Assertions resulting in a strong internal control environment are considerably more reliable than a weak or non-existent internal control environment.

Sufficiency and Appropriateness of Audit Evidence Evaluation

The sufficiency and appropriateness of audit evidence refers to the quantity and quality of such evidence, respectively. The quantity of evidence needed varies inversely according to the risk of material misstatement, though if the quality of evidence is greater—if the evidence is more appropriately fitted to bear on the attempted conclusion—then the required quantity of evidence can be decreased. The auditor must exercise professional judgment in determining the reliability of obtained evidence to be sufficient and appropriate for the conclusions reached.

Documentation Accords with Professional Standards Evaluation

Since the Sarbanes-Oxley Act of 2002, auditor accountability and independence has been a crucially important element of an auditor's work. One means of maintaining the auditor's professional accountability is through the mandatory compliance of his work with professional standards; his documentation must be in accordance with standards for the auditing professions. Having layers of authority helps to ensure that the auditor responsibly does his work while maintaining independence.

Auditors to Review Others' Work

Part of an auditor's responsibility to the client company is that he cannot abdicate his duties to others; he can delegate duties, but his delegation of duties must be accompanied by his oversight and review. Even when an auditor seeks a specialist to aid him in the audit of the client company, he should review the specialist's reasoning and conclusions to assess their fairness and accuracy. This is especially true for subordinate and other auditors on the audit team.

Audits Involving More Than One Auditor

Methods Used by Auditors to Obtain Credibility of the Other Auditor and the Method for the Auditor to Make Reference to the Other Auditor in the Audit Report

In situations where more than one auditor audits an entity and provides an opinion, the standard report may need to be altered. An example would be an auditor auditing a large company, but another auditor auditing a small subsidiary. The principal auditor auditing the entire company will probably need to give an opinion on the financial statements of the consolidated entity. In this situation, the principal auditor will need to obtain credibility for the auditor auditing the subsidiary. Therefore, it is a requirement that the principal auditor perform the following:

1. Inquire as to the other auditor's reputation. One method of doing this is by contacting professional accounting organizations.
2. Obtain evidence of independence from the other auditor.
3. Verify that the other auditor is knowledgeable regarding the applicable reporting framework (e.g. GAAP) and GAAS and that he is aware that his report will be included with the principal auditor's report.

a. Should the principal auditor not be satisfied with the results of research on the other auditor, he may need to consider altering the audit report or auditing the subsidiary. When a principal auditor decides to make reference to the audit of another auditor, the principal auditor's report should clearly indicate the division of responsibility between that portion of the financial statements covered by the audit of the principal auditor and that covered by the audit of the other auditor.

Guidelines the Auditor Must Follow to Name the Other Auditor and the Auditor's Assumption of Responsibility for the Other Auditor's Work

When there are multiple auditors associated with auditing one entity, a division of responsibility must be considered. If the principal auditor desires to mention the other auditor by name in the overall audit report, the principal auditor must do to the following:

1. Get the other auditor's permission to disclose the other auditor's name
2. In the audit report, state the value audited by the other auditor (in terms of revenues or assets)
3. Present the other auditor's report.
    a. If the principal auditor does not desire to mention the other auditor in the audit report, the principal auditor should issue the standard report. In doing so, the principal auditor is assuming responsibility of the other auditor's work. Instances of this include when the other auditor is affiliated with the principal auditor, when the other auditor audited an immaterial portion of the consolidated company, or when the other auditor was hired by the principal auditor. However, the principal auditor should perform at least one of the following actions:
        i. Visit with the other auditor
        ii. Review the other auditor's audit programs
        iii. Review the other auditor's work papers
        iv. Conduct additional audit procedures

Uncorrected Misstatements and Related Conclusions

An auditor typically expects the client company to correct any material misstatements or substantial control deficiencies which provide a risk of material misstatement, though this is not always the case. He therefore should document whatever misstatements are left uncorrected and be sure to know the claimed reasons behind the inability or unwillingness of the company to correct them, as well as the reasons for the existence of the misstatement itself. This could lead him to other and larger conclusions related to the rest of his audit for the client company.

A Going Concern Issue

An auditor may issue an unmodified report with an emphasis-of-matter or other-matter paragraph when there is a **going concern** issue. The auditor must decide if there is substantial doubt as to whether the company can continue as a going concern for a time period not to exceed one year from the financial statement date. Often the auditor will have substantial doubt if the company has difficulty meeting financial obligations, significant legal contingencies, or similar problems. If there is **substantial doubt** that the company can continue based on auditing procedures, the auditor must review the plans of management and determine the likelihood that these plans will be successful. If the auditor still has substantial doubt, the auditor must decide if the financial statement disclosures have properly disclosed this issue; additionally, the auditor must issue either a disclaimer or an unmodified report with an explanatory paragraph. In both cases, the auditor *must* include the terms "substantial doubt" and "going concern."

MANAGEMENT'S DISCUSSION AND ANALYSIS (MD&A)

Management's discussion and analysis (MD&A) is part of a company's annual report where the management provide an overview of the company's past and present operations, analyzing how the company fared in the previous year and what directions the company might take moving forward.

The auditor ought to examine and report upon the MD&A, determining whether it accords with SEC requirements, whether its data is accurate, and whether its conclusions are reasonable. An audit of MD&A helps to provide users with greater assurance.

RETAINING AUDIT DOCUMENTATION

Audit documentation needs to be retained not merely for the ordinary business practices of the auditor (where he might need to find old files upon a client's request), but also to comply with established legal regulations. Sarbanes-Oxley requires that auditors retain the documentation necessary to support their opinions on the client for seven years following the audit.

PREPARING COMMUNICATIONS WITH MANAGEMENT

An auditor's communication with management is central to the success of his audit. He ought to remain in contact with them, not only to request information and to make inquiries for the audit, but also to evaluate their performance himself. After evaluating them, an auditor might see it fit to document his findings and suggestions for improvement (if there are any) in a **management letter**. This letter can help management to make advancements in their operations or controls.

More particularly, the auditor is required to communicate with management at least once per year to remind them of the terms of the audit engagement; he also must document this reminder.

REPORTS ON AUDITED FINANCIAL STATEMENTS

Since an auditor's main purpose is to audit financial statements, a significant document is his report on audited financial statements.

According to AU 508, all such reports must contain a title including the word "independent," an assertion expressing that the client's financial statements were audited, a statement noting the ultimate responsibility of management for the financial statements and the responsibility of the auditor to provide his opinion, a declaration that the audit was conducted in accordance with US GAAS, a statement that such standards require the auditor to provide reasonable assurance of the financial statements' reliability, a statement that the audit includes an examination of evidence supporting financial statement items, an assessment of accounting principles followed to reach those assertions, and an overall evaluation of the financial statement's presentation, a declaration that the auditor believes his audit provides reasonable grounds for his opinion, an opinion concerning the accuracy of the financial statements, the auditor's signature, and the report's date.

SAMPLE AUDIT REPORT FOR A STANDARD UNMODIFIED OPINION

INDEPENDENT AUDITOR'S REPORT

To: The XYZ Company Board of Directors and Stockholders.

We have audited the accompanying balance sheets of XYZ Company as of December 31, 20XX and 20XX, and the related statements of income, retained earnings, and cash flows for the years then ended. These financial statements are the responsibility of the Company's management. Our responsibility is to express an opinion on these financial statements based on our audits.

We conducted our audits in accordance with US generally accepted auditing standards. Those standards require that we plan and perform the audit to obtain reasonable assurance about whether the financial statements are free of material misstatement. An audit includes examining, on a test basis, evidence supporting the amounts and disclosures in the financial statements.

In our opinion, the financial statements referred to above present fairly, in all material respects, the financial position of XYZ Company as of December 31, 20XX and 20XX, and the results of its operations and its cash flows for the years then ended in conformity with US generally accepted accounting principles.

John Doe, CPA Washington, D.C. 2/1/2014

Government Auditing Standards

Generally accepted government auditing standards (GAGAS), also known as the **Yellow Book**, are comprised of five general standards governing independence, due care, continuing professional education, supervision, and quality control. These standards are utilized for audits of federal government organizations and at other levels of government as well.

Auditors are responsible for reporting any deficiencies they uncover in their work to the appropriate officials, including their recommended solutions and other pertinent information. Some information might need to be omitted, if it is not allowed to be publicly disclosed; and if so, the auditor should note that in his report. Auditors may also limit those to whom the report is distributed for similar reasons.

Compliance with Laws and Regulations Reports

An important goal for modern companies is regulatory compliance, their conformity to the relevant laws and regulations which affect or govern their operations. Consequently, an important goal for auditors is to ensure that their client companies conform to the required legislation. An auditor should include in his report any deficiencies that his client has in terms of regulatory compliance, whether those deficiencies are control deficiencies that give rise to a risk of violating regulations, or whether they are violations in themselves.

Internal Control Reports

Auditors are generally required not only to offer an opinion on the quality, fairness, and accuracy of the financial statements themselves, but also to assess and provide commentary upon a company's internal controls over financial reporting. An auditor should therefore seek to identify weaknesses in a company's internal controls, spotting weaknesses that create a risk for material misstatement. These risks need to be documented in the auditor's reports when he provides his commentary on internal controls, as well as recommended solutions and the management's compliance in correcting them.

Processing of Transactions by Service Organizations Reports

Service auditors are required to provide reports on the processing of transactions by service organizations, which are the organizations providing servces to user organizations. Service auditors are required to maintain independence from the service organizations, but not necessarily from user organizations.

The service auditor can issue either a report on controls placed in operation, or a report on controls placed in operation and tests of operating effectiveness. Both report the design effectiveness of internal controls that were placed in operation as of a given date, and the latter also reports on their operating effectiveness. Auditors can also issue special-purpose reports, which outline the nature and purpose of the engagement and auditor's opinion.

AGREED-UPON PROCEDURES REPORTS

Agreed-upon procedures are procedures requested by a client for an auditor to fulfill, in which the auditor analyzes and offers commentary upon the requested subject matter. The content of these procedures are agreed upon by the client and the auditor beforehand, hence their name.

Reports on agreed-upon procedures must disclose the nature of the engagement, a statement that the responsibility of the effectiveness and appropriateness of the audited procedures is ultimately with the company (not the auditor), a description of the auditor's procedures he performed and his findings, the level of materiality he calculated and utilized, a disclaimer that the auditor did not necessarily do the work required for an all-things-considered opinion (and thus that there could be certain relevant information which he would have noticed with a more extensive audit), a restriction on the use of the report for the client company's purposes, any limitations or reservations on the auditing procedures utilized in the audit, and a description of any specialists employed in the audit.

FINANCIAL FORECASTS AND PROJECTIONS

Financial forecasts are prospective financial statements which aim to present a company's financial position, results of operations, and cash flows as they are expected to be at some future date, whether in terms of specific amounts or within a range.

Financial projections are prospective financial statements which aim to present a company's financial data given specific courses of action or specific events' taking place.

AT 301 provides CPAs with guidance concerning their activities in assessing, creating, or applying agreed-upon procedures to financial forecasts and financial projections.

PRO FORMA FINANCIAL INFORMATION REPORTS

***Pro forma* financial information** aims to show how historical financial information would have been different if some event had occurred or if some course of action had been taken.

AT 101 and AT 401 provide guidance for the assessment and creation of *pro forma* financial statements. Any audit of *pro forma* financial information should include the auditor's assessment of the assumptions made by management and the different events or branches of the company that would have been affected by the hypothetical past event. The auditor should ensure that presentations of *pro forma* financial information indicate the need to read such information in conjunction with the actual historical financial data for the firm.

SPECIAL REPORTS

An auditor can issue a number of special reports. These include (1) reports for financial statements that he audits which conform to some other comprehensive basis of accounting, (2) reports for audits on particular items or elements of a financial statement, (3) reports for audits which assess the compliance of a client company with contractual or regulatory requirements pertaining to their audited financial statements, (4) reports for financial presentations which, after having conformed to contractual or regulatory requirements, are incomplete or out of conformity with the applicable reporting framework, and (5) reports on financial data which have been presented according to prescribed forms or schedules.

Reissued Reports

Reissued reports are comparative financial statements issued subsequent to the date of the original report but nonetheless displaying the same date as the original report. If the report is revised due to the effects of certain events between the original date and the date of its reissuance, it should be duel-dated, meaning that the original date must be noted in addition to the date of the relevant events.

Internal Control Matters in the Audit

In an auditor's evaluation of the client company's internal controls, he should seek to not only locate control deficiencies but also judge the degree of their severity: how much they provide a risk for misstatement. SAS 112 provides guidance to auditors in their evaluation of the severity of control deficiencies and also states the obligation of auditors to communicate significant deficiencies and material weaknesses to management and to those charged with governance.

Communication with Those Charged with Governance

The auditor is required to stay in communication with those charged with governance over the client company. He should make known to them the uncorrected misstatements which he identified in the audit, as well as whatever bearing they have on his audit opinion. He should also ask that such misstatements be resolved, informing those charged with governance of the effects of their failure to correct such misstatements. The auditor should also inform those charged with governance of the bearing that uncorrected misstatements for priod periods have upon present (and future) financial statement items.

The auditor ought to document all misstatements, known or likely, that have been corrected, and the reasons for those left uncorrected, including an evaluation of such reasons.

Subsequent Discovery of Facts Existing at the Date of the Auditor's Report

Sometimes the auditor may, after the date of his audit report, become aware of facts pertaining to relevant circumstances existing at the date of the report. In such a case, the auditor should quickly attempt to investigate more about the nature and relevance of such facts. He should discuss it with management to request permission and with a lawyer to discuss possible legal implications of continuing the audit following the date of the audit report.

If the auditor sees that such new facts would significantly alter certain financial information, he should advise his client to provide a disclosure of the new facts and their bearing on financial statement users. If the client does not comply, then the auditor should inform the board of directors, telling them that without the client's cooperation, his audit report will not be associated with the company's financial statement and that he will inform relevant regulatory agencies and users of the change.

Omitted Procedures After the Report Date

Sometimes the auditor may, after the date of his audit report, become aware of procedures that he ought to have performed by the date of the report. He is not thereby obligated to perform the needed procedures, although there should be an appropriate disclosure in the auditor's reports and work papers, and he should determine whether or to what degree the absence of such a procedure affects the audit opinion he issued. If there is a significant difference arising from the absence of the procedure, then he should seek to apply the omitted procedures; and if he is unable to do so, then he should consult a lawyer to determine his responsibilities to the client, to regulatory authorities, and to financial statement users.

Attestation Standards guidance for reports

Attestation Standards provide guidance on the following reports:

1. **Agreed-upon procedures** – the report consists of the procedures that were conducted and the resulting findings
2. **Attestation** – can include breakeven analysis, compliance with regulations, corporate governance, historical events, internal control, performance measurements, etc.
3. **Financial projections and forecasts** – forms include compilation, examinations, and agreed-upon procedures; a financial projection is based on a hypothetical assumption and shows possible results; a financial forecast shows expected results of a future accounting period based on future conditions that are expected
4. Management discussion and analysis – included in annual
5. reports sent to stockholders and in reports filed with the SEC
6. **Pro forma financial information –** adjusts prior historical financial information prospectively to reflect transactions that may be proposed or that may have occurred

Underwriter letters

Underwriter letters are often used by public companies attempting to issue new securities to the general public. The auditor will be engaged to produce a "comfort" letter on prospectus financial information. The auditor will usually provide positive assurance that the auditor is independent and that the audit was in compliance with SEC standards. The "comfort" letter will also give negative assurance on an assortment of accounting issues (for example, *pro forma* financial information).

Accounting principles applications is when accountants may be engaged by a prospective client to report, either orally or in writing, on the application of specific accounting principles for a prospective or completed transaction. The accountants are required to consult with the company's current auditor and to understand the transaction.

Clarity Project

The **Clarity Project** is a comprehensive undertaking to both clarify auditing standards and align the US GAAS with the International Standards on Auditing (ISAs). This change occurs specifically within the Statements on Auditing Standards (SASs) in the auditing (AU) section of the AICPA *Professional Standards*, expanding the body of original SASs with extra Clarified SASs that supersede certain previous SASs. (In other words, the Clarity Project aims not to alter previous SASs but to write entirely new ones which supersede specific older ones.)

The biggest content changes, rather than mere semantic changes, in the Clarified SASs involve (1) the authority of the ten fundamental standards of GAAS, (2) the naming and format of an auditor's report, and (3) the standards for group audits, i.e. audits of grouped companies.

Ten fundamental standards of GAAS

The General Standards, Standards of Fieldwork, and Standards of Reporting comprise the ten fundamental standards of GAAS. Per the Clarified SASs, these rules are no longer to be treated as authoritative standards as such, but are instead to provide a general framework explaining a proper audit, with the more specific details of the SASs incorporating these ten rules and having authority in themselves. The Clarified SASs refer to these ten rules as "clarified principles."

Auditor's Report

Naming and Format

While the previous SASs referenced auditors' reports as either "qualified" or "unqualified," referring to whether the auditor wished to qualify his approval of the company's financials with some other observation, the Clarified SASs use the terminology "modified" and "unmodified," presumably to remove the connotation of personal or professional qualifications.

The Clarified SASs also establish a specific format for both the unmodified report and the modified report.

Format of an Unmodified Auditor's Report

An unmodified audit report must have the following sections, each with its own heading:

1. **Title** (must include word "independent")
2. **Introductory paragraph**
    a. must identify entity, state that it's been audited, and specifiy date or period for which audit applies
3. **Description of management's responsibility**
    a. asserts that management is responsible for preparing and fairly presenting financials according to "applicable reporting framework" (e.g. IFRS or GAAP), and management's responsibility over the design, implementation, and maintenance of internal control
4. **Auditor's responsibility**
    a. asserts that the audit was performed per US GAAS, asserts that audits are designed to obtain "reasonable assurance" of financials' reliability, and describes audit, including procedures performed
5. **Audit opinion** – includes unqualified/unmodified opinion

Format of a Modified Audit Report

A modified audit report must have the following sections, each with its own heading (note that only (5) differs from the unmodified report):

1. **Title** (must include word "independent")
2. **Introductory paragraph**
    a. must identify entity, state that it's been audited, and specify date or period for which audit applies
3. **Description of management's responsibility**
    a. asserts that management is responsible for preparing and fairly presenting financials according to "applicable reporting framework" (e.g. IFRS or GAAP), and management's responsibility over the design, implementation, and maintenance of internal control
4. **Auditor's responsibility**
    a. asserts that the audit was performed per US GAAS, asserts that audits are designed to obtain "reasonable assurance" of financials' reliability, and describes audit, including procedures performed
5. **Basis for modified opinion**
6. **Audit opinion** – may include qualified/modified opinion, adverse opinion, or disclaimer of opinion

Emphasis-of-matter (EOM)

An **emphasis-of-matter** (EOM) paragraph refers to some matter included in the entity's financial statements to which the auditor wishes to draw the reader's attention; an **other-matter** (OM) paragraph is similar but refers to some matter *outside* the statements. Both of these paragraphs are to involve issues which require the reader's attention but are insufficiently weighty to merit a modified opinion by themselves (although other issues could still cause a modified opinion). Previously such matters were included in the *explanatory paragraph* of the audit report.

EOM and OM paragraphs should immediately follow the audit opinion paragraph in an audit report, and all EOM paragraphs should precede all OM paragraphs.

Examples of issues deserving an EOM or OM paragraph would be a going concern issue, an updated report from a prior period, a catastrophic event, a litigation uncertainty, unusual subsequent events, etc.

If the auditor includes an EOM or OM paragraph, he must communicate the matter to those charged with governance prior to including it in the report.

Clarified Statements on Auditing Standards (SASs)

The Clarified SASs refer to any audit of consolidated financial statements (e.g. financials for a parent and subsidiaries) as a **group audit**, and has changed some of the terminology. Previously the head auditor for such an audit was called the "principal auditor," but now he is the *group engagement auditor*. "Engagement partners" are now *group engagement partners*, and "other auditors" (i.e. auditors for different discrete entities in the group) are now "component auditors."

Group engagement team and group engagement auditor

The **group engagement team** – composed of the group engagement auditor, the group engagement partners, and various staff – is responsible for planning the overall audit strategy for the grouped entities, including communicating with any component auditors and understanding their component audits. They are also particularly responsible for establishing the materiality threshold for the component auditors, and establishing it at a lower level than the materiality threshold for the group audit as a whole.

The **group engagement auditor** is responsible for the direction, supervision, and performance of the group audit engagement as a whole, along with the audit report.

Work of a component auditor

The **component auditor's** work depends on the significance of the component to the grouped entities considered as a whole.

If the component is significant due to financial materiality, the component auditor must audit the component's financial information.

If the component is significant due to a risk of material misstatement, then audit procedures must be performed, but not a full audit of the component's particular financials.

If the component is non-significant, then audit procedures at the group level must be performed.

Accounting and Review Services Engagements

Accounting and Review Services

Whereas auditing services provide reasonable assurance that financial statements conform to the applicable reporting framework (e.g. GAAP) and are accurate and complete, **accounting services** can consist of managing a company's payables and receivables, keeping track of their payroll, and overseeing the company's bookkeeping (maintaining the ledgers, reconciling bank statements, and other things), in addition to tax services. **Review services** are more closely related to audits, though they are still distinct. A review seeks to provide "limited assurance," seeking to identify significant matters related to the financial statements, but not assessing all the matters a full audit would cover, such as internal controls or comprehensive tests of accounting records.

Statements on Standards for Accounting and Review Services (SSARS)

Statements on Standards for Accounting and Review Services (SSARS) give guidance to auditors on writing compilations and reviews for unaudited financial information; the statements are issued by the AICPA. There are also interpretive publications which provide additional guidance concerning the practical application of SSARS, even though such publications are not authoritatively binding, as the SSARS themselves are, though a CPA needs to justify a departure from interpretive guidance. There are also other publications for compilation and review services, but CPAs do not need to be aware of them, and they are even less authoritative than the interpretive publications.

Attest Services, Assurance Services, and Consulting Services

Attest services occur when the CPA receives a written assertion that is the responsibility of another party. The CPA will provide a conclusion pertaining to the reliability of the written assertion. Audits are included in attest services. Attestation general standards include independence, training, performance, and professional knowledge of the subject matter. Attestation fieldwork standards include sufficient planning, evidence, and supervision. GAAS is less in scope than attestation standards.

According to the AICPA's Special Committee on Assurance Services, **assurance services** are "independent professional services that improve the quality of information, or its context, for decision makers." All attestation services are included in assurance services; assurance services also include risk assessment, information systems reliability, the measurement of business performance, and the measurement of health care performance.

Consulting services are when the CPA and the client develop and agree on the nature of the work to be performed. The CPA then formulates the findings and conclusions accordingly. The CPA also makes recommendations to the client based on the findings.

Professional Responsibilities

AICPA Code of Professional Conduct

The AICPA **Code of Professional Conduct** is based on ethics in philosophy, and its authority is derived from the bylaws of the AICPA. It is specific as to what is permissible for CPAs and applies to all AICPA members. CPAs need a code of professional conduct due to the need and desire to control actions and behavior of the members for the good of the profession and society. It is also needed to enable CPAs to gain public confidence in the quality of service. It is imperative for CPAs to maintain a high level of integrity. The Code does have similarities to other professions, such as its prohibition of discreditable acts and requirement of competence.

A difference between the CPA's Code and other professions' required ethics is the issue of independence. The profession of public accounting has deemed it essential to promulgate the Code and to establish a mechanism for enforcing observance of the Code, since a distinguishing mark of a profession is its acceptance of responsibility to the public.

Code compliance mainly relies upon the AICPA members' understanding of the Code and their actions taken voluntarily. Once this is taken into consideration, Code compliance may secondarily rely on peer reinforcement, disciplinary proceedings (CPAs may receive admonishment, up to two years of suspension, AICPA expulsion, or acquittal), and the opinion of the public.

Articles

Article I asserts that CPAs should exercise sensitivity in their moral and professional judgments and that they have responsibilities not only to their own clients but also to other CPAs. All CPAs ought to be good representatives of CPAs in general.

Article II specifies CPAs' obligation to serve the public interest and to accept its serious responsibility to the public.

Article III concerns the integrity which CPAs ought to have, especially with respect to CPAs' honesty with their clients and commitment to confidentiality. A commitment to service and to the public must be above one's personal benefit.

Article IV requires independence of the CPA for services of auditing and attestation, and objectivity for all services provided by CPAs. Independence consists of avoiding conflicts of interest, and CPAs ought to maintain it both in fact and in appearance.

Article V concerns CPAs' obligation to exercise due care, striving for excellence and competence in the services one provides.

Article VI involves the scope and nature of services provided by CPAs. When assessing the scope and nature of services for prospective clients, CPAs should ensure that such services would not impair their independence or professionalism.

Auditor's Independence

It does not compromise an auditor's independence to provide recommendations or advice as an aid to the client company's management, but a number of services do, such as having the authority to complete or document transactions for the client, possessing client assets, supervising workers of the client company, determining which of one's own recommended courses of action will be taken, addressing the board of directors on management's behalf, providing financial services to the company, and creating or maintaining the client's system of internal controls.

Independence Standards Boards (ISB) statements

ISB 1 concerns the auditor's independence discussions with audit committees. According to this pronouncement, the auditor is required to inform the audit committee of all his relationships that have bearing on the question of his independence, discuss his independence with the committee, and state his judgment concerning his own independence. The auditor's relationships and judgment of his own independence must be submitted in writing.

ISB 3 concerns those who become employed with companies who were formerly audit clients, since there are questions involving the objectivity of the auditor prior to leaving his first company and the reluctance of the current auditors to express appropriate skepticism when dealing with a former co-worker. According to this pronouncement, before leaving the firm, an auditor must disclose any conversations he has had with the client over possible employment, so that the objectivity of his work can be reviewed. After an auditor is employed with a former client, extra caution must be given to preserve the audit team's objectivity. If an auditor joins a former client within one year of leaving his audit firm and then significantly interacts with the audit team, the subsequent annual audit needs to be reviewed by someone who was not involved in the prior audit.

ISB 2 is still in effect but not relevant to the CPA exam.

Auditor responsibilities to his clients

An auditor is responsible to his clients to maintain appropriate confidentiality. An auditor should not disclose information about a client except with his consent. The only times an auditor may do so without the client's consent is if a subpoena, government regulation, or professional practice review procedure requires it, or if the auditor has a complaint with an investigative body or a lawsuit against the client.

An auditor is also prohibited from entering into an agreement where his pay is contingent on the results of his assessment of the client company, though contingent fees are sometimes allowed for the provision of tax services.

Acts discreditable to the profession

Auditors' acts which are discreditable to the profession include the retention of a client's records after he has requested them from the auditor, practices of discrimination and harassment, a failure to comply with appropriate standards and procedures in government audits, negligence in the preparation of financial information, a failure to comply with the obligations imposed by government bodies, the solicitation or disclosure of questions from the CPA exam, and a failure to fulfill one's own tax obligations.

Consulting services of auditors standards

The **Management Consulting Services Executive Committee** of the AICPA issues various **Statements on Standards for Consulting Services** (SSCS). In addition to these standards, a number of guiding principles are contained within the AICPA Code of Professional Conduct, especially Rule 201 and Rule 202.

Public Company Accounting Oversight Board (PCAOB)

The **Public Company Accounting Oversight Board** (PCAOB) was established by SOX to prevent the self-regulation of public accounting. There are a number of PCAOB provisions, including the requirements for auditing firms (1) to retain the workpapers needed to support audit opinions for seven years following the audit, (2) to have a second partner review and approve audit reports, (3) to have standards for quality control among registered public accounting firms, (4) to assess and report on the client management's evaluation of internal controls in an internal control report, (5) to rotate lead audit or coordinating partners every five years, and (6) to discuss with the client's audit committee the utilization of accounting policies and the implications of doing otherwise.

Sarbanes-Oxley Act (SOX)

Besides establishing the PCAOB, which is itself overseen by the SEC, the Sarbanes-Oxley Act (SOX) seeks to preserve auditor independence by forbidding registered public accounting firms from additionally giving certain nonaudit services to their clients, including bookkeeping services, design for financial information systems, appraisal or valuation, actuarial services, internal audit outsourcing services, management or human resources, financial services, legal services, and others.

SOX also requires that audit committees for client companies be in charge of hiring and overseeing the work of external audit companies, including the preapproval of permissible nonaudit activities by the external audit company.

Title II, Title III, and Section 303

Title II of SOX is comprised of nine sections outlining the auditor's obligations to remain independent, including requirements on the approval of new auditors, the rotation of audit partners, and the restriction of certain nonaudit services by the audit firm.

Title III is comprised of eight sections outlining the individual responsibility of the client entity's senior executives for the completeness and accuracy of the company's financial presentations.

Section 303 forbids the improper influence of officers, directors, or anyone under them to fraudulently influence or manipulate public accountants in an attempt to materially misstate financial information.

Government Accountability Office (GAO)

The **Government Accountability Office** (GAO) publishes rules governing the independence and ethics of auditors who provide services under the auspices of generally accepted government auditing standards (GAGAS). GAO standards are comprised of two primary principles concerning the performance of nonaudit services: (1) that nonaudit services provided cannot include management functions or decisions and (2) that audit firms cannot audit their own work or perform nonaudit services when such services would be materially related to audits they are performing.

For the most part, GAO standards and AICPA standards are equivalent, since both employ a principles-based approach to evaluating the independence of the provision of some service. In other respects, however, GAO standards are stricter, such as having certain restrictions over the firm's ability to post transactions or provide human resources services for the client.

Department of Labor (DOL)

The **Department of Labor** (DOL) is a cabinet department of the federal government in the US, overseeing employee-related issues such as unemployment insurance benefits, occupational safety, re-employment services, and standards for wages and hours worked. Therefore, DOL standards largely apply to auditors who are assessing various employee benefit plans. These standards seek to provide guidelines for auditor independence.

IFAC Code of Ethics for Professional Accountants

The **International Federation of Accountants** (IFAC) is a global accounting organization which represents 2.5 million accountants in 124 different countries. IFAC includes the **International Ethics Standards Board for Accountants** (IESBA), which issues the **Code of Ethics for Professional Accountants**. This code lays out various ethical obligations for professional accountants, with sections on integrity, objectivity, professional competence, confidentiality, threats to and safeguards for objectivity and independence, conflict resolution, and issues for public practice (such as scope, conflicts of interest, marketing services, custody of client assets, etc).

In the cases where domestic regulations keep accounting professionals from complying with this code of ethics, such professionals are nonetheless required to comply with the remainder of the code.

IFAC Code of Ethics Threat Categories and Safeguards

Threat categories include **self-interest** (leading to a conflict of interests), **self-review** (where an accountant can be too lenient in reviewing himself or a coworker), **advocacy** (where an accountant will promote his client or employer's position to such an extent that his objectivity is compromised), **familiarity** (that an enduring relationship with a client or employer harms objectivity), and **intimidation** (where pressures keep an accountant from retaining objectivity).

Safeguards for the elimination of threats include (1) those safeguards created by the profession or by legislation, such as educational requirements to enter the profession, regulations of corporate governance, and disciplinary procedures within the profession, and (2) safeguards within the work environment, which seek to mitigate the formation of interests that might compromise one's objectivity.

Systems of Quality Control

It is crucial that auditing firms craft for themselves **quality control standards** which establish policies and procedures related to the attest practice of the firm in general and of individual auditors in particular. Quality control systems ought to be conducive towards the goal of a firm's compliance with established attestation standards, but engagements can still be performed in conformity with such professional standards even if the quality control system is deficient or if the auditors fail to comply with that system.

Quality Control

Peer Reviews, Documentation Maintenance, and Professional Development

In a **peer review**, other CPAs (or peers) will review and determine the quality of the firm's accounting and audit work. Quality control standards provide guidelines for peer reviews. Peer reviews motivate auditors to conduct high-quality audits because the audits may be selected for review, and they can also locate low-quality audit procedures. Self-regulation can be cost-effective versus the alternative of government regulation. In connection with the element of monitoring, a CPA firm's system of quality control should ordinarily provide for the maintenance of documentation to demonstrate compliance with its policies and procedures.

One element of the personnel management quality control standard is professional development. The primary reason a CPA firm establishes policies and procedures for professional development of staff accountants is to provide reasonable assurance that staff personnel will have the knowledge required to enable them to fulfill responsibilities. Evidence of the CPA firm's adherence to prescribed standards of quality control can include a CPA firm's personnel partner studying the

CPA firm's personnel advancement experience periodically to determine whether individuals meeting stated criteria are assigned increased degrees of responsibility.

Titles I and IV of the Sarbanes-Oxley Act

Title I of SOX establishes the Public Company Accounting Oversight Board (PCAOB), which maintains great supervision over auditors and auditing firms. It is comprised of nine sections.

Title IV involves "enhanced financial disclosures," outlining the reporting requirements for corporate officers' stock transactions, *pro forma* financial information, off-balance sheet transactions, and other financial transactions. The section also requires internal controls for these disclosures. It is comprised of nine sections as well.

Terms

AUDIT TERMS

Access controls: restrict access to program documentation, files of data, computer hardware, and computer programs to authorized employees; examples include passwords and locks

Adverse opinion: an opinion expressing that financial statements as a whole do not conform with the applicable reporting framework

Audit trail: a record of transaction flow from beginning (supporting documentation) to end (the financial statements), or from end to beginning

Audit scope: the range of activities covered by an audit. Audit scope includes, where appropriate, the audit objectives, the nature and extent of auditing procedures performed, the time period audited, and any related activities not audited in order to delineate the boundaries of the audit.

Audit work schedules: include what activities are to be audited; when they will be audited; and the estimated time required, taking into account the scope of the audit work planned and the nature and extent of audit work performed by others.

Audit working papers record the information obtained, the analyses made, and the conclusions reached during an audit. Audit working papers support the bases for the findings and recommendations to be reported.

CAAT: computer assisted auditing techniques

Conclusions: the auditor's evaluations of the effects of the findings on the activities reviewed. Conclusions usually put the findings in perspective based upon their overall implications.

Crossfoot: numbers are summed both vertically and horizontally to see that they are accurate.

Cross-reference: in cases of the same information being documented on two different workpapers, the auditor will notate the reference of each workpaper on the other workpaper.

Current workpaper files: contains supporting documentation for the audit.

Disclaimer: a statement that the auditor is unable to express an opinion as to the presentation of financial statements in conformity with the applicable reporting framework

Disclosure: revealing information; financial statement footnotes are one way of providing necessary disclosures.

Dual date: if a major event comes to the auditor's attention between the report date and issuance of the report, the financial statements may include the event as an adjustment or disclosure. The auditor dual dates the audit report (as of the end of fieldwork, except for footnote XX, which is dated later).

Earnings per share: stockholder profit for each share of stock owned

EDI: "Electronic Data Interchange," the use of communication between an entity and customers or suppliers to transact business electronically. Purchasing, shipping, billing, cash receipts, and cash disbursements can be completed entirely by exchanging electronic messages.

External auditors: those audit professionals who perform independent annual audits of an organization's financial statements.

Flowchart: a representation, primarily through the use of symbols, of the sequence of activities in a system (process, operation, function, or activity)

Footnote: located at the end of the financial statements; pertains to the financial statements

GASB: Government Accounting Standards Board, the entity that develops governmental accounting standards

Generalized audit software: packaged computer programs used to process audit functions

Hardware controls: built-in computer controls on computer equipment

Immaterial: insignificant; would not alter any financial decisions

Index: arrangement of letters and/or numbers assigned to a workpaper for reference purposes

Integrated test facility: set up to test the client's computer system by utilizing a "dummy" department to test processing data simultaneously with "real" client data

Lead schedule: The schedule at the beginning of audit documentation that summarizes the detailed schedules

Manual controls: controls that are done manually, not by computer

Misstatement: inaccurate financial statement information

Monitoring: encompasses supervising, observing, and testing activities and appropriately reporting to responsible individuals. Monitoring provides an ongoing verification of progress toward achievement of objectives and goals

Negative assurance: informs the information user that the auditor has not discovered anything to reflect that the financial information is inaccurate

Negative confirmation: requests that the recipient respond only if the information is inaccurate

Objectives: the broadest statements of what the organization chooses to accomplish

Objectivity: an independent mental attitude which requires auditors to perform audits in such a manner that they have an honest belief in their work product and that no significant quality compromises are made. Objectivity requires auditors not to subordinate their judgment on audit matters to others'.

Operations: the recurring activities of an organization directed toward producing a product or rendering a service; such activities may include, but are not limited to, marketing, sales, production, purchasing, human resources, finance and accounting, and governmental assistance

Operating effectiveness: how an internal control was applied, the consistency with which it was applied, and by whom

Opinion: a CPA's conclusion held with confidence but not substantiated by positive knowledge or proof

Parallel simulation: client data is processed with audit software; the auditor's results are compared with the client's results in processing the same data; used to test the client's computer system

Pervasive: having the ability to permeate. An error is pervasive if it is material to more than one of the primary financial statements.

Permanent workpapers: permanent audit documentation containing information of continuing accounting significance; this information is updated annually

Positive confirmation: requests that the recipient confirm the accuracy of an item

Predecessor auditor: a client's most recent former auditor

Modified opinion: the auditor's opinion that, "except for something," the financial statements are fairly presented

Reasonableness Test: a comparison of an estimated amount, calculated by the use of relevant financial and non-financial information, with a recorded amount

SAS: Statements on Auditing Standards, performance standards issued by the AICPA Auditing Standards Board

Scope limitation: a restriction that precludes the auditor from accomplishing the audit goals and objectives. A scope limitation results from a lack of evidence, such as an inability to conduct an audit procedure considered necessary. For example, if the client had an equity investment in a foreign affiliate and the auditor is unable to obtain audited financial statements for the affiliate, the auditor does not have sufficient appropriate evidence to determine the amount of equity income or the reported amount of the investment account.

Significant audit findings: those conditions which, in the judgment of the auditor, could adversely affect the organization. Significant audit findings may include conditions dealing with irregularities, illegal acts, errors, inefficiency, waste, ineffectiveness, conflicts of interest, and control weaknesses.

SSAE: Statements on Standards for Attestation Engagements developed by the AICPA

SSAR: Statements on Standards for Accounting and Review services; performance standards issued by the AICPA Accounting and Review Services

Successor auditor: the external auditor who becomes the auditor after the predecessor auditor

Supervision: a continuing process, beginning with planning and ending with the audit conclusion; includes providing suitable instructions to subordinates and approving the audit program, seeing that the approved audit program is fulfilled unless deviations are justified and authorized, determining that audit workpapers adequately support findings, conclusions, and reports, and making sure that audit reports are accurate, objective, clear, concise, constructive, and timely

System (process, operation, function, or activity): an arrangement, set, or collection of concepts, parts, activities, and/or people that are connected or interrelated to achieve objectives and goals; applies to both manual and automated systems; may also be a collection of subsystems operating together for a common objective or goal

Unmodified opinion: an opinion indicating that the auditor believes that the financial statements are fairly presented

Working trial balance: contains accounts with the current year-end balances; has columns for adjustments, reclassifications, and final balances

How to Overcome Test Anxiety

Just the thought of taking a test is enough to make most people a little nervous. A test is an important event that can have a long-term impact on your future, so it's important to take it seriously and it's natural to feel anxious about performing well. But just because anxiety is normal, that doesn't mean that it's helpful in test taking, or that you should simply accept it as part of your life. Anxiety can have a variety of effects. These effects can be mild, like making you feel slightly nervous, or severe, like blocking your ability to focus or remember even a simple detail.

If you experience test anxiety—whether severe or mild—it's important to know how to beat it. To discover this, first you need to understand what causes test anxiety.

Causes of Test Anxiety

While we often think of anxiety as an uncontrollable emotional state, it can actually be caused by simple, practical things. One of the most common causes of test anxiety is that a person does not feel adequately prepared for their test. This feeling can be the result of many different issues such as poor study habits or lack of organization, but the most common culprit is time management. Starting to study too late, failing to organize your study time to cover all of the material, or being distracted while you study will mean that you're not well prepared for the test. This may lead to cramming the night before, which will cause you to be physically and mentally exhausted for the test. Poor time management also contributes to feelings of stress, fear, and hopelessness as you realize you are not well prepared but don't know what to do about it.

Other times, test anxiety is not related to your preparation for the test but comes from unresolved fear. This may be a past failure on a test, or poor performance on tests in general. It may come from comparing yourself to others who seem to be performing better or from the stress of living up to expectations. Anxiety may be driven by fears of the future—how failure on this test would affect your educational and career goals. These fears are often completely irrational, but they can still negatively impact your test performance.

Elements of Test Anxiety

As mentioned earlier, test anxiety is considered to be an emotional state, but it has physical and mental components as well. Sometimes you may not even realize that you are suffering from test anxiety until you notice the physical symptoms. These can include trembling hands, rapid heartbeat, sweating, nausea, and tense muscles. Extreme anxiety may lead to fainting or vomiting. Obviously, any of these symptoms can have a negative impact on testing. It is important to recognize them as soon as they begin to occur so that you can address the problem before it damages your performance.

The mental components of test anxiety include trouble focusing and inability to remember learned information. During a test, your mind is on high alert, which can help you recall information and stay focused for an extended period of time. However, anxiety interferes with your mind's natural processes, causing you to blank out, even on the questions you know well. The strain of testing during anxiety makes it difficult to stay focused, especially on a test that may take several hours. Extreme anxiety can take a huge mental toll, making it difficult not only to recall test information but even to understand the test questions or pull your thoughts together.

Effects of Test Anxiety

Test anxiety is like a disease—if left untreated, it will get progressively worse. Anxiety leads to poor performance, and this reinforces the feelings of fear and failure, which in turn lead to poor performances on subsequent tests. It can grow from a mild nervousness to a crippling condition. If allowed to progress, test anxiety can have a big impact on your schooling, and consequently on your future.

Test anxiety can spread to other parts of your life. Anxiety on tests can become anxiety in any stressful situation, and blanking on a test can turn into panicking in a job situation. But fortunately, you don't have to let anxiety rule your testing and determine your grades. There are a number of relatively simple steps you can take to move past anxiety and function normally on a test and in the rest of life.

Physical Steps for Beating Test Anxiety

While test anxiety is a serious problem, the good news is that it can be overcome. It doesn't have to control your ability to think and remember information. While it may take time, you can begin taking steps today to beat anxiety.

Just as your first hint that you may be struggling with anxiety comes from the physical symptoms, the first step to treating it is also physical. Rest is crucial for having a clear, strong mind. If you are tired, it is much easier to give in to anxiety. But if you establish good sleep habits, your body and mind will be ready to perform optimally, without the strain of exhaustion. Additionally, sleeping well helps you to retain information better, so you're more likely to recall the answers when you see the test questions.

Getting good sleep means more than going to bed on time. It's important to allow your brain time to relax. Take study breaks from time to time so it doesn't get overworked, and don't study right before bed. Take time to rest your mind before trying to rest your body, or you may find it difficult to fall asleep.

Along with sleep, other aspects of physical health are important in preparing for a test. Good nutrition is vital for good brain function. Sugary foods and drinks may give a burst of energy but this burst is followed by a crash, both physically and emotionally. Instead, fuel your body with protein and vitamin-rich foods.

Also, drink plenty of water. Dehydration can lead to headaches and exhaustion, especially if your brain is already under stress from the rigors of the test. Particularly if your test is a long one, drink water during the breaks. And if possible, take an energy-boosting snack to eat between sections.

Along with sleep and diet, a third important part of physical health is exercise. Maintaining a steady workout schedule is helpful, but even taking 5-minute study breaks to walk can help get your blood pumping faster and clear your head. Exercise also releases endorphins, which contribute to a positive feeling and can help combat test anxiety.

When you nurture your physical health, you are also contributing to your mental health. If your body is healthy, your mind is much more likely to be healthy as well. So take time to rest, nourish your body with healthy food and water, and get moving as much as possible. Taking these physical steps will make you stronger and more able to take the mental steps necessary to overcome test anxiety.

Mental Steps for Beating Test Anxiety

Working on the mental side of test anxiety can be more challenging, but as with the physical side, there are clear steps you can take to overcome it. As mentioned earlier, test anxiety often stems from lack of preparation, so the obvious solution is to prepare for the test. Effective studying may be the most important weapon you have for beating test anxiety, but you can and should employ several other mental tools to combat fear.

First, boost your confidence by reminding yourself of past success—tests or projects that you aced. If you're putting as much effort into preparing for this test as you did for those, there's no reason you should expect to fail here. Work hard to prepare; then trust your preparation.

Second, surround yourself with encouraging people. It can be helpful to find a study group, but be sure that the people you're around will encourage a positive attitude. If you spend time with others who are anxious or cynical, this will only contribute to your own anxiety. Look for others who are motivated to study hard from a desire to succeed, not from a fear of failure.

Third, reward yourself. A test is physically and mentally tiring, even without anxiety, and it can be helpful to have something to look forward to. Plan an activity following the test, regardless of the outcome, such as going to a movie or getting ice cream.

When you are taking the test, if you find yourself beginning to feel anxious, remind yourself that you know the material. Visualize successfully completing the test. Then take a few deep, relaxing breaths and return to it. Work through the questions carefully but with confidence, knowing that you are capable of succeeding.

Developing a healthy mental approach to test taking will also aid in other areas of life. Test anxiety affects more than just the actual test—it can be damaging to your mental health and even contribute to depression. It's important to beat test anxiety before it becomes a problem for more than testing.

Study Strategy

Being prepared for the test is necessary to combat anxiety, but what does being prepared look like? You may study for hours on end and still not feel prepared. What you need is a strategy for test prep. The next few pages outline our recommended steps to help you plan out and conquer the challenge of preparation.

Step 1: Scope Out the Test

Learn everything you can about the format (multiple choice, essay, etc.) and what will be on the test. Gather any study materials, course outlines, or sample exams that may be available. Not only will this help you to prepare, but knowing what to expect can help to alleviate test anxiety.

Step 2: Map Out the Material

Look through the textbook or study guide and make note of how many chapters or sections it has. Then divide these over the time you have. For example, if a book has 15 chapters and you have five days to study, you need to cover three chapters each day. Even better, if you have the time, leave an extra day at the end for overall review after you have gone through the material in depth.

If time is limited, you may need to prioritize the material. Look through it and make note of which sections you think you already have a good grasp on, and which need review. While you are studying, skim quickly through the familiar sections and take more time on the challenging parts.

Write out your plan so you don't get lost as you go. Having a written plan also helps you feel more in control of the study, so anxiety is less likely to arise from feeling overwhelmed at the amount to cover.

Step 3: Gather Your Tools

Decide what study method works best for you. Do you prefer to highlight in the book as you study and then go back over the highlighted portions? Or do you type out notes of the important information? Or is it helpful to make flashcards that you can carry with you? Assemble the pens, index cards, highlighters, post-it notes, and any other materials you may need so you won't be distracted by getting up to find things while you study.

If you're having a hard time retaining the information or organizing your notes, experiment with different methods. For example, try color-coding by subject with colored pens, highlighters, or post-it notes. If you learn better by hearing, try recording yourself reading your notes so you can listen while in the car, working out, or simply sitting at your desk. Ask a friend to quiz you from your flashcards, or try teaching someone the material to solidify it in your mind.

Step 4: Create Your Environment

It's important to avoid distractions while you study. This includes both the obvious distractions like visitors and the subtle distractions like an uncomfortable chair (or a too-comfortable couch that makes you want to fall asleep). Set up the best study environment possible: good lighting and a comfortable work area. If background music helps you focus, you may want to turn it on, but otherwise keep the room quiet. If you are using a computer to take notes, be sure you don't have any other windows open, especially applications like social media, games, or anything else that could distract you. Silence your phone and turn off notifications. Be sure to keep water close by so you stay hydrated while you study (but avoid unhealthy drinks and snacks).

Also, take into account the best time of day to study. Are you freshest first thing in the morning? Try to set aside some time then to work through the material. Is your mind clearer in the afternoon or evening? Schedule your study session then. Another method is to study at the same time of day that you will take the test, so that your brain gets used to working on the material at that time and will be ready to focus at test time.

Step 5: Study!

Once you have done all the study preparation, it's time to settle into the actual studying. Sit down, take a few moments to settle your mind so you can focus, and begin to follow your study plan. Don't give in to distractions or let yourself procrastinate. This is your time to prepare so you'll be ready to fearlessly approach the test. Make the most of the time and stay focused.

Of course, you don't want to burn out. If you study too long you may find that you're not retaining the information very well. Take regular study breaks. For example, taking five minutes out of every hour to walk briskly, breathing deeply and swinging your arms, can help your mind stay fresh.

As you get to the end of each chapter or section, it's a good idea to do a quick review. Remind yourself of what you learned and work on any difficult parts. When you feel that you've mastered the material, move on to the next part. At the end of your study session, briefly skim through your notes again.

But while review is helpful, cramming last minute is NOT. If at all possible, work ahead so that you won't need to fit all your study into the last day. Cramming overloads your brain with more information than it can process and retain, and your tired mind may struggle to recall even previously learned information when it is overwhelmed with last-minute study. Also, the urgent nature of cramming and the stress placed on your brain contribute to anxiety. You'll be more likely to go to the test feeling unprepared and having trouble thinking clearly.

So don't cram, and don't stay up late before the test, even just to review your notes at a leisurely pace. Your brain needs rest more than it needs to go over the information again. In fact, plan to finish your studies by noon or early afternoon the day before the test. Give your brain the rest of the day to relax or focus on other things, and get a good night's sleep. Then you will be fresh for the test and better able to recall what you've studied.

Step 6: Take a Practice Test

Many courses offer sample tests, either online or in the study materials. This is an excellent resource to check whether you have mastered the material, as well as to prepare for the test format and environment.

Check the test format ahead of time: the number of questions, the type (multiple choice, free response, etc.), and the time limit. Then create a plan for working through them. For example, if you have 30 minutes to take a 60-question test, your limit is 30 seconds per question. Spend less time on the questions you know well so that you can take more time on the difficult ones.

If you have time to take several practice tests, take the first one open book, with no time limit. Work through the questions at your own pace and make sure you fully understand them. Gradually work up to taking a test under test conditions: sit at a desk with all study materials put away and set a timer. Pace yourself to make sure you finish the test with time to spare and go back to check your answers if you have time.

After each test, check your answers. On the questions you missed, be sure you understand why you missed them. Did you misread the question (tests can use tricky wording)? Did you forget the information? Or was it something you hadn't learned? Go back and study any shaky areas that the practice tests reveal.

Taking these tests not only helps with your grade, but also aids in combating test anxiety. If you're already used to the test conditions, you're less likely to worry about it, and working through tests until you're scoring well gives you a confidence boost. Go through the practice tests until you feel comfortable, and then you can go into the test knowing that you're ready for it.

Test Tips

On test day, you should be confident, knowing that you've prepared well and are ready to answer the questions. But aside from preparation, there are several test day strategies you can employ to maximize your performance.

First, as stated before, get a good night's sleep the night before the test (and for several nights before that, if possible). Go into the test with a fresh, alert mind rather than staying up late to study.

Try not to change too much about your normal routine on the day of the test. It's important to eat a nutritious breakfast, but if you normally don't eat breakfast at all, consider eating just a protein bar. If you're a coffee drinker, go ahead and have your normal coffee. Just make sure you time it so that the caffeine doesn't wear off right in the middle of your test. Avoid sugary beverages, and drink enough water to stay hydrated but not so much that you need a restroom break 10 minutes into the test. If your test isn't first thing in the morning, consider going for a walk or doing a light workout before the test to get your blood flowing.

Allow yourself enough time to get ready, and leave for the test with plenty of time to spare so you won't have the anxiety of scrambling to arrive in time. Another reason to be early is to select a good seat. It's helpful to sit away from doors and windows, which can be distracting. Find a good seat, get out your supplies, and settle your mind before the test begins.

When the test begins, start by going over the instructions carefully, even if you already know what to expect. Make sure you avoid any careless mistakes by following the directions.

Then begin working through the questions, pacing yourself as you've practiced. If you're not sure on an answer, don't spend too much time on it, and don't let it shake your confidence. Either skip it and come back later, or eliminate as many wrong answers as possible and guess among the remaining ones. Don't dwell on these questions as you continue—put them out of your mind and focus on what lies ahead.

Be sure to read all of the answer choices, even if you're sure the first one is the right answer. Sometimes you'll find a better one if you keep reading. But don't second-guess yourself if you do immediately know the answer. Your gut instinct is usually right. Don't let test anxiety rob you of the information you know.

If you have time at the end of the test (and if the test format allows), go back and review your answers. Be cautious about changing any, since your first instinct tends to be correct, but make sure you didn't misread any of the questions or accidentally mark the wrong answer choice. Look over any you skipped and make an educated guess.

At the end, leave the test feeling confident. You've done your best, so don't waste time worrying about your performance or wishing you could change anything. Instead, celebrate the successful completion of this test. And finally, use this test to learn how to deal with anxiety even better next time.

Review Video: Test Anxiety
Visit mometrix.com/academy and enter code: 100340

Important Qualification

Not all anxiety is created equal. If your test anxiety is causing major issues in your life beyond the classroom or testing center, or if you are experiencing troubling physical symptoms related to your anxiety, it may be a sign of a serious physiological or psychological condition. If this sounds like your situation, we strongly encourage you to seek professional help.

Online Resources

Due to our efforts to try to keep this book to a manageable length, we've created a link that will give you access to all of your online resources:

mometrix.com/resources719/cpaauditing

It's Your Moment, Let's Celebrate It!

Share your story @mometrixtestpreparation